BONZO

BILLY BONDS

BONZO

AN AUTOBIOGRAPHY

ARTHUR BARKER
A division of Weidenfeld Publishers Limited
London

Published in Great Britain by
George Weidenfeld & Nicolson Limited
91 Clapham High Street
London SW4 7TA

Printed and bound in Great Britain by
Butler & Tanner Ltd, Frome and London

To my wife Lyn, children Claire and Katie, and my mum and dad . . . to all of whom I owe so much.

Illustrations

The 'closed door' Cup-tie (*Steve Bacon*)
The nearest I ever got to a cap (*FA official photograph*)
Last of the summer wine (*Steve Bacon*)
With Len Cearns and John Lyall (*Steve Bacon*)
The card school (*Steve Bacon*)
Geronimo rides again (*Steve Bacon*)
Cut-glass vase (*Steve Bacon*)
The PFA Merit Award (*Bob Thomas*)
A day none of the family will ever forget (*Royal rota photograph*)
Coast-to-coast coverage with NBC (*Steve Bacon*)

The photographs in this book come from the author's collection unless otherwise stated.

Acknowledgements

My sincere thanks to Trevor Smith. We have known each other a long time now and share many memories, the recalling of which has given us both a lot of pleasure, and I am most grateful for all his help in putting this book together.

I would also like to thank Colin Downey, Football Association Referees' Secretary; Stanley Searl, former Sports Editor, *Mansfield Chronicle and Advertiser;* and Colin Cameron, official Charlton Athletic statistician and historian.

1

A fine May evening, ninety minutes after the final whistle, claret-and-blue ribbons on the FA Cup, and Wembley all but deserted. The thousands who had earlier packed the ground to see Second Division West Ham win the 1980 final by the only goal against First Division London rivals Arsenal were well on their various ways to a Saturday night knees-up they'd remember the rest of their lives.

Which is exactly what I was doing at that particular moment ... remembering.

I'd slipped out of the mad-house which was Hammers' dressing-room, walked back up the players' tunnel, and stood gazing round the silent, empty stadium. I wanted those few moments to myself, just me and my thoughts.

For it was the second time Billy Bonds had enjoyed the great privilege of leading West Ham United to an FA Cup final triumph. Five years earlier we'd won the trophy in another all-London final when, as a Division One club, we beat Second Division Fulham. And it was not until after that great day was over that I suddenly realised I had no proper recollection of it whatever. The whole occasion was simply a blur in my mind: getting up in our hotel on the day of the final, making the coach trip to Wembley, receiving the cup, the lap of honour ... none of it came back to me.

So when we returned there in 1980 I was determined that second chance was not going the same way. This time I was doing my best to take in everything that happened throughout the day and imprint it on my mind for ever.

That's why I left the noisy, jubilant West Ham dressing-room and returned on my own for a last look at the arena. 'You may not be back here again – so make the most of it,' I told myself, content to just stand there and let my eyes wander slowly about the vast ground.

The usual post-match litter blew around the terraces, where

the sweepers were already clearing up. Dotted about here and there were small groups of fans, doing much the same as I was, I suppose. Maybe some were enjoying a verbal play-back of our goal – a rare strike from my great mate Trevor Brooking. But it wasn't the day's action I dwelt on. It seemed I already had the whole ninety minutes of that mentally taped.

Before I went back down the tunnel so many famous players had used, I thought for a moment about other days in an empty football ground, more than twenty years earlier, when the week's high spot for a sixteen-year-old Billy Bonds was the Friday afternoon spent getting the Valley pitch ready for Charlton's match the next day.

As a humble groundstaff boy then, that was among my regular jobs, and always the one I enjoyed most. It may sound daft, but to me there was something almost beautiful about being out there in the big, empty ground, handpainting in the white pitch markings with everyone else gone, apart from us few groundstaff hopefuls and groundsman Jack Myton. Even on a bleak, grey mid-winter day, with the light fading fast, it never failed to get to me.

Those long-ago Fridays are as vivid to me now as that deserted Wembley evening after we'd done the Gunners. From The Valley to Wembley isn't far as the crow flies – but for me it was a long, long way in football terms.

2

There are a great many people I owe a lot to for helping me in my football career over the years. But it has to begin with my mum and dad.

I was the first of their three children. Our old house opposite Woolwich Ferry is now no longer there. Where it used to stand is a green, part of redevelopment in the area.

My dad, Arthur, worked on maintenance for London Transport. My mum, Barbara, was very much the typical wife and mother of those days. I cannot remember her ever not being there when my brother Michael, sister Linda and I came home.

That kind of secure family background is the best possible start in life for children. It has left me with an in-built appreciation of proper values, which see you through the hardest knocks. You take it all for granted at the time, of course, but I know now just how important it is to grow up in such a caring atmosphere. My happiest moments these days are being at home with my wife Lyn and our own two girls.

I was lucky, too, to have a dad who was sport mad and a mum equally enthusiastic. The family album boasts one snapshot of Dad with Mick a baby in his arms and me by his side with a football at my feet . . . all of two years old!

Dad was a good footballer, a winger useful enough to play for London Transport. He picked up loads of medals until a broken leg ended his playing days. He was also a great Charlton follower, dating back to pre-war years when The Valley was regularly crammed for First Division games.

There was a lot to follow Charlton for then. Under the legendary Jimmy Seed, the club had climbed from Third to First Division in successive pre-war seasons and then appeared in the first two FA Cup finals after the war.

In view of later events, it's worth telling how my dad managed to see both of those finals.

They got a few tickets where he worked, but nowhere near

enough to go round. So it was decided they would be allocated on the toss of a coin. He called right both times! Charlton, of course, broke a few hearts by crashing 4–1 to Derby County in the first final, but beat Burnley with a Chris Duffy goal when they went back again the next season.

Mum was as keen a football fan as Dad, and regularly accompanied him to Charlton home games. In fact, I was very nearly born on the Valley terraces!

People like mine never went in for sitting in the stands – money was too tight for that – so Mum and Dad were in their usual place on the terrace for one game, with her in what must have been a very advanced stage of pregnancy with me. The game was hardly over before she told Dad they ought to get to the maternity hospital a bit sharpish. I actually arrived at ten o'clock the next morning ... that near to being at a football match on my very first day in the world!

And it wasn't much longer before I *was* there. My own first memories of watching Charlton are of being perched throughout a match on Dad's shoulders, when little more than a toddler. But Mum tells me they first took me when I was only three months old. She held me in her arms, again standing on the terrace, but doesn't now recall if I upset anyone with my bawling!

When I was about four years old the family moved to The Vista, at Eltham, SE9. My first school was King's Park, and later I went to Middle Park Junior School.

I wasn't a particularly big lad but by the age of nine was in the school team, even though the rest of the side were a couple of years my senior. It was a good team, with ten of the eleven also in the Woolwich district Under-11 squad, including me. But I must be honest – we didn't win anything at that level.

I virtually lived for football. My game was very much a 'follow-the-ball' affair of chasing all over the place and trying to get hold of it before them.

The Bonds brothers were constantly together. Because of the two-year age difference, we never played in the same school team or Sunday morning side, but were regular team-mates in the daily after-school kick-abouts and also in the Magpies, our estate five-a-side squad.

The Sunday morning club we both played for was Moatbridge – and it was through them I had my first-ever contact with Bobby Moore. Moatbridge were a very successful team, well run by a Mr Flowers. We paid a tanner a week subs which, among other things, went to pay for hiring the school hall for training one night each week.

When Moatbridge won their championship, Mr Flowers marked the occasion by arranging – don't ask me how – for Mooro to visit us and present the cup and medals. For me, at the age of thirteen or fourteen, it was just about the biggest thing that had ever happened.

Bobby could not have been much over twenty himself, but he was like a movie star to us that night. Already an England Youth and Under-23 star, he was widely accepted as among the game's greatest prospects.

He arrived in a marvellous suit and accompanied by his wife Tina. We looked at the suit and that beautiful wife – and were simply struck dumb! After we went up one by one and received our medals, Bobby and Tina were treated to an exhibition of dribbling skills by us kids. You can imagine, it never entered my young head that, one day, I would be his team-mate and eventually follow him as Hammers' skipper!

After I got to West Ham I mentioned that night to Mooro and asked him if he remembered handing me a medal and shaking my hand. He recalled going across the river into Kent for a presentation evening with a boys' club . . . but I don't think he could honestly place me there.

Mick followed me to The Valley, doing the same Tuesday and Thursday evening training with the juniors as I had earlier. He was a good prospect but perhaps did not have quite the same committed approach. Some weeks he'd do the Tuesday but miss out on the Thursday. But while we were always close, I never got on to Mick about that kind of lapse. He was his own man, with his own life to lead the way he saw it. It would have been great if we had ended playing together for Charlton. But I never pushed Mick's chances at the club – not that anyone would have taken much notice of what a mere groundstaff kid like me thought, anyway.

3

At school we had some excellent teachers who put in a lot of time with us at football. I remember a Mr Fishington and a Mr Collins as particular influences for me.

It must have been with one of those two that I received my first trophy as team skipper. Middle Park deposed old rivals Wyborne Junior School as champs, and one afternoon I was let off school work to go with a master in his car over to Wyborne and bring back the cup.

From the time I got into the school team Dad was much involved, arranging his work rota so he could be on the touchline at most Saturday morning games. As a fair player himself there was none of the 'frustrated footballer' father about him. Any advice or criticism was constructive – and to this day if he feels I've not done as well as I might he merely says, 'That's one to forget, Bill.' But he was always positive I would make it in the game. 'You can be a player ... if you work really hard at it,' was his regular comment.

When I progressed to Eltham Green Comprehensive School my first six weeks of senior school sport were spent playing rugby. You got a similar period of soccer later and then decided which you wanted to concentrate on. Usually, I played scrum-half, and quickly developed almost as much enthusiasm for rugger as I had for soccer. But it was the latter we played all the time out of school hours.

On our estate car owners were few, so it was easy and safe to get a pick-up game going in the street any time, with either a tennis ball or a polythene football. It didn't please everyone to have a crowd of shouting kids kicking a ball about at all hours, but if nothing else we learned to be quick off the mark! When the ball went sailing into a front garden, you had to be over the fence or through the gate and grab it before someone rushed out to clump your head.

Mostly, though, we cheerfully ignored by-laws by putting our coats down on the inviting greens in front of various nearby blocks of flats, despite the 'no ball games' council notices. These games were regularly halted by the arrival of the Old Bill, summoned by an irate tenant. 'Come on you lot, that's not allowed,' he'd growl, clearing us off the green. We'd slope away round the nearest corner, wait until he'd gone, and then go back and take up where we'd left off!

What with those hours, plus house games, inter-school matches on Saturday and playing for a Sunday morning junior club, my life revolved around football. Academically, I must have been something of a trial to my teachers. I still remember one forcefully informing me in front of the whole class: 'Your brains, Bonds, are all in your feet!'

It's a judgement I cannot argue with.

4

By my early teens I was going to Charlton matches with Mick rather than with our parents. The two of us would invariably meet up with our mates in the same spot on the ground every game, right by the halfway line.

The Charlton line-up those days included Willie Duff in goal, John Hewie, Derek Ufton, John Sewell, Brian Kinsey, Billy Kiernan, Ron White – brother of Spurs' brilliant John White – and Johnny Summers. Some of the games we watched seem unbelievable now. I recall a 7–6 win against Huddersfield and a 6–6 draw with Middlesbrough.

But keen as I was, it was football as a game that interested me rather than the players. I was never one for chasing autographs, hanging around for a glimpse of a first-team star, or for having a particular idol I tried to model myself on. What happened out there on the park was my main concern, and I studied the opposition's tactics as much as Charlton's.

This general interest in the game also took me across the river a couple of times to West Ham, when West Brom and Burnley were the visitors. I forget what happened in the Albion game, but the Turf Moor team slammed Hammers 5–2.

In school football I was chosen for Kent, playing either centre-half or what we then called wing-half. We played a goal-less draw with Essex at Walthamstow Avenue, and won 3–2 against a Middlesex side including two who would be future team-mates at West Ham – Harry Redknapp and John Sissons.

Another game was against Sussex on a sloping pitch. We had this and a strong wind behind us first half and went in 3–1 up ... only to lose finally 8–3!

There were always pro club scouts around district and Sunday morning games, just as there are today. But it was playing five-a-sides with the Magpies which led to me going to Charlton. Mum tells me now that I went home after one such outing and told her, 'That man was there again, watching us, Mum.'

'That man' turned out to be Jock Basford, who was then coach at The Valley. It wasn't long before he had a chat with Dad, and as a result I was invited to go to Charlton twice a week, Tuesday and Thursday evening, training with their juniors.

What we did does not compare with the intensive coaching youngsters receive with pro clubs these days. Our evenings were largely spent lapping the pitch and doing physical work, with very little emphasis on skills. But for the young Billy Bonds it was the first foot on the ladder.

5

When I left school at fifteen it was with a far from impressive academic record – and very little idea of what I was going to do, other than play football. While never a real dunce in the class-room, I suspect teachers really earned their money with me. I cannot honestly regret they were not more successful, because I believe you learn a great deal anyway as you go through life. But I frankly admit I'm totally baffled now by our girls' homework!

I could have gone on Charlton's groundstaff straight away, but Dad was dead set against that. He insisted I should get a trade behind me first – a very sensible attitude when you think of how many don't make it in the game.

Talks with the school careers officer brought up possibilities like the police or fire brigade. I suspect Dad would have approved of either for me, if only because both carried a pension!

But finally it was at Stone's factory, almost opposite The Valley, where I began my working life. They made things like ships' propellors, and I was indentured there for four or five years as a fitter/turner at two pounds ten shillings a week. I was never so miserable in all my life! There was nothing wrong with the factory or the people, but all I seemed to do was make tea and run errands.

After a couple of months Dad saw how fed up I was, had a talk with Frank Hill, then Charlton's manager, and to my great relief I came out of the factory and joined the Valley groundstaff. Once there, I was soon making cups of tea again ... and sweeping the terraces, cleaning boots and drying kit, too. And as at the factory, I still rode to work on my bike. Mick and I both had bikes for Christmas presents some years earlier, gifts that enabled us to take on paper rounds. For fifteen bob a week, getting up at six every morning was well worth it!

I firmly believe those few months of factory work were crucial in turning me into a pro footballer. It was just the gee-up I needed to make me put everything into it ... because no way was I ever going back to a work bench.

There was little glamour about being a groundstaff boy, though. After training, when all the senior players had left, you had to do your share of the menial chores. Jack Myton made sure you did them right, too.

Us kids were always fair game for the Charlton pros, who did not hesitate to give us stick. I was literally scared stiff of going into the dressing-room while they were there. If it was my turn to collect the dirty training kit, I'd try and sneak in unnoticed, grab it up off the floor and rush out to the drying-room before they saw me. I rarely succeeded. John Hewie, the tall South African defender who played for Scotland, particularly enjoyed ragging me. It was all done in a joking way, with nothing nasty about it, but for a fifteen-year-old Billy Bonds, naturally a bit introverted, a real ordeal. John probably sussed this out, because his favourite trick was to make me towel his back dry when he came out of the showers – while he gave a running commentary upon my performance in training and likely prospects in the game.

A couple of years or so later John lost his first-team place to me ... and was among the first to wish me well on my debut.

6

Lyn still shudders now if I start on about what it was like at Charlton for us in those days.

The Valley was already an old ground then, and the main stand a rat-infested place. But the groundstaff lads regularly took their lunch-time sandwiches down into the boiler-room under the stand, and thought nothing of it.

And, like any other job, there were little perks. The real bunce for us was sweeping up after matches. It was a bad day when you did not wind up three or four bob better off from the coins you unearthed under all the litter. Best area was along the front of the stand, where the fumbled pennies and threepenny bits rolled when fans bought programmes and eats and drinks. On what we were getting, it was a welcome, tax-free bonus!

The groundstaff boys saw quite a lot of manager Frank Hill – though not in relation to our football progress.

There was a snooker table in the Valley board-room, covered over and used as a table on match days. Most afternoons Frank would 'hustle' us a tanner a time. The flooring in there was pretty uneven, so the table had one or two 'rolls'. Frank knew them inside out from long practice – and regularly relieved us of our money. You couldn't argue with the boss, could you?

Football-wise, I owe him little. He rarely said anything to me about my game, one way or the other. One day he watched a match I played in at Bexley. Dad happened to be there as well, and Frank Hill told him: 'Your lad will never be a footballer – he's like a donkey.'

It was as well for me that Dad waited a few years before passing on that particular verdict!

Fortunately for me, what my then manager thought did not really matter. Jock Basford, the man who had first spotted me in those council estate five-a-side games, was still coach at The Valley and gave me nothing but help and encouragement. A quiet, modest man with a deep knowledge of the game, Jock was the one who put me firmly on the right road. One day he told me: 'Billy, I'm sure you are more of a right-back than a right-half.' The change of position paid off almost at once.

But I still believe it was only Jock's insistence to Frank Hill that later earned me a first-team chance.

7

Before that day came, however, there was plenty of work for me to put in on my game at youth and reserve team levels. Playing in the first team was then only something I occasionally dreamed about.

For a couple of seasons I played mainly in the youth or A team, with an infrequent reserve outing. One of these was in the old London Challenge Cup. The pro clubs used their reserve sides in this competition, but the top amateur teams also took part. Charlton played at Plough Lane against Wimbledon, who were then in the Isthmian League – and they beat us 3–1.

Youth and A team games were played either at The Valley or on Standard Cables ground at New Eltham. For away matches we went in an old motor coach, a real throw-back to charabanc days. It had Charlton Athletic Football Club plastered all over it in big letters, but was such a banger the club would have done better to keep quiet about who it belonged to! We got used to having to get out and push to get it going, or to the nearest garage. I don't think we ever actually failed to reach our destination, but once, when we were desperate to get back to The Valley for a vital relegation game in the afternoon, the bus broke down and by the time we had shoved it miles to a garage we had missed almost all of the first half.

I was still playing youth, A team and reserve football in 1964 when the FA Cup third round draw was made. We heard it on the radio, hoping like everyone else for an easy game ... and groaned when Charlton came out of the hat away to West Ham. 'That's it for another season,' we moaned.

It was, too. Hammers fans will need no reminding that their side stuffed us 3–0 at Upton Park – and went on to win the Cup for the first time.

After getting on for a thousand senior outings I recall very little of those early seasons of reserve football. Nor do I recollect much about the day I was told, for the first time, that I was in the first team. Mum and Dad reckon now that I rushed home pretty excited about it. Not much past eighteen at the time, I suppose I must have also been a bit apprehensive. For my debut game was against Northampton Town at The Valley.

Under the old Arsenal wing-half Dave Bowen, the Cobblers had created a stir by moving in successive seasons from Division Four to Division Two. The day of my debut they came to us top of the table, on their way to the First Division.

Charlton were toiling well down the division, which I suppose is why the manager thought something had to be done and brought me in. One of my youth team friends had already beaten me to the senior side – Ray Keeley, who'd had a couple of games in midfield and who I was to run into on another, later occasion.

The thought of getting my own debut did not exactly worry me. After all, it was this I'd been striving hard for all along. But one of Northampton's stars was Scots winger Tommy Robson, formerly with Chelsea ... and he was the man a green-as-grass Billy Bonds had to mark.

The game was different then. Full-backs marked wingers man-to-man, with nobody helping out in front or tucking in round the back like they do now. You either got the better of them or they made you look a monkey.

Dave Bowen had Northampton well organised. Theo Foley was playing for them then, in a defence which had the off-side trap worked out a treat. But we got a 1–1 draw, and I must have done a reasonable job against the experienced, tricky Robson. At the finish I was quietly satisfied with how it had gone for me.

My parents naturally were there for my debut, along with Mick – this time the Bonds family having complimentary seats in the stand – and they all felt I'd done well.

The rude awakening was not long coming. I was in again the next Saturday against Southampton at The Dell. We were crucified 4–0, with a lad called George O'Brien getting all four goals. It was a real hiding, but just look at the attack Saints had: John Sydenham, Martin Chivers, George O'Brien, Jimmy Melia and Terry Paine. What price a front line like that in Division Two these days?

Once again, the manager had to do something and he did ... by dropping me! It was an obvious gambit, opting for experience over promise in such a situation. But to this day it remains the only time in my career that I have been dropped. The versatile John Hewie, whose place I'd taken at right-back, had stayed in the side elsewhere, and when I got the chop reverted to his usual number two spot. But Charlton lost their next game, 3–1 at home to Bolton. And I was promptly recalled.

We played Coventry at Highfield, when Jimmy Hill was the boss there and present Coventry manager John Sillett their right-back. George Curtis, now overall top man with the Sky Blues, played centre-half. It was a bruising encounter and we lost 2–1. Coventry, pushing hard for promotion, were accused afterwards by our guv of trying to kick their way into Division One. I marked Dave Clements, a big, blond forward, and gave as good as I got, I think.

I finished that season with thirteen games to my credit and, apart from injury, never went out of the side again. The following season I missed only two League games and was ever-present the next.

8

All the time I was learning – particularly from my mistakes. Some still have me wincing now when I remember them. Playing Plymouth at The Valley we were leading 1–0 with about fifteen minutes left. The ball was knocked over my head down the line, but I turned and was well first to it. Their bloke rushed up to close me down and I thought I'd be clever and knock it past him instead of doing the obvious and hoofing the ball up the back of the stand. He nicked it off me, went by, crossed, and they scored. I trudged off at the end acutely aware I'd cost us a point.

Playing it simple was something Jock Basford was always impressing on us. I remember one rucking from him for not doing that in a reserve game. 'What on earth did you want to try that for?' he demanded. 'If you can play it simple, do it every time. Just knock it off the way you are facing if there's somebody there for it.'

There's still no better advice.

Another early clanger of mine which still gives me nightmares came against Portsmouth at Fratton Park. It brought me the fastest goal I've ever scored ... only problem was that it went in my own net! Pompey kicked off and scalped a big, high ball down the line towards me. I glanced it back with my head to our goalkeeper, only then realising he had come well off his line. The ball sailed clean over him and we were one down – with the official time given as twenty seconds!

What made it even worse was that our goalkeeper Les Surman, a former youth squad mate, was having his senior debut. Micky Rose and Noel Dwyer, the usual first and second choices, were out injured or something. What a start for poor Les! We ended up losing 3–1. But it was a necessary part of the learning process for me. Errors of that kind I was determined never to repeat.

Fratton Park proved to be a bad ground for me. The following season I collected a badly broken nose there. It resulted from one of those really horrible balls for defenders: a high, deep cross over your head towards the back post. I moved backwards intending to head away – just as Pompey's Denis Edwards came steaming in behind me.

Denis had previously been at Charlton and we'd played together many times. He was a husky lad, with a notably big forehead. It was this part of his anatomy which caught me full in the face as I half turned towards him. I went down with my hooter in a rare mess. As I was helped off, blood streaming, I honestly thought it had been knocked clean off.

I got a reminder of that painful occasion only last season in 1987–88 when I was back at Fratton Park with West Ham. Because of injuries, I'd been called into the squad for the first time, but I did not play and watched the game from the bench. As I sat there a chap obviously connected with Pompey came up and asked if I remembered him. When I confessed I did not, he told me: 'I was one of the guys who helped you when you got your nose broken here with Charlton.' So all those years later I thanked him – since, having other things on my mind, I don't suppose I did at the time.

I still have the large piece of cartilage the surgeon removed from my nose when I had an operation to repair the damage later on.

It's funny how a certain ground can definitely become a jinx place for you. Fratton Park still is as far as I'm concerned. I managed to have a run-in with the ref there not long ago – in a pre-season friendly. And only last season I was in a West Ham reserve side that got stuffed 5–2!

9

I remember once running across the Hammers on our travels during those days in the Charlton first team. We'd been playing at Notts County and went home by train, eating sandwiches in our second-class compartment, as usual. When the train reached London we saw a crowd of excited fans massing round the door of a first-class carriage further down the platform.

We realised who they were mobbing when Bobby Moore, John Byrne, Geoff Hurst and Jack Burkett got off the train. We saw how they travelled in style, with a restaurant car all to themselves. Dressed to the nines, collar and tie, carrying suit covers, they were obviously all set for a night on the town. It was so different to humble Charlton, and there was certainly plenty of envy in me as I thought: 'What a flash crowd of ******* they are!'

Charlton had their own stars, of course, among them Ron Saunders, a real bull of a centre-forward who would run all day and was totally fearless. My first glimpse of Ron came some seasons before. We went down to Fratton Park for a youth game, but it was called off. Rather than waste the whole day, the Charlton youth side stayed on to watch Portsmouth hammer Newcastle 5–2 in the afternoon – with Ron getting a hat-trick against a Magpies team including Bob Stokoe.

For all his power and aggression on the field, Ron was a smashing bloke. A model pro, he set a fine example and was always ready with helpful advice to me. I admired him as a player and liked him as a man.

There'd been a change of manager at The Valley by the time Ron arrived there. Frank Hill's services were dispensed with – and his departure lost me no sleep. Bob Stokoe came from Bury to take over, and his arrival proved good news for me. By then, I had gained popularity with the Charlton crowd because of my hundred per cent attitude, and I think that put me in well with Bob from the start.

He could be a frightening character. He had those steely eyes that seem to bore right through you, and it was not a pleasant experience to be on the receiving end of a rucking from him.

Bob also hated losing ... at anything, not merely first team football. If his side got beat in our five-a-side games he was in a foul mood afterwards. Those matches were played on the car park at Charlton. The surface was merely pounded down cinder and small stones, but Bob never pulled any punches with his tackling. One side of the 'pitch' was bordered along its length by the concrete wall of a public toilet, and more than once I was sent smashing into that by a Stokoe challenge, never mind about the risk of injury putting you out of action! Yet Bob always ordered that nobody touched a ball on the day before a game. He only ever allowed lapping the pitch and a few sprints, declaring we must save our legs for the next day.

It was a happy time for me. I achieved a consistent standard of performance and, while my only concern was playing well for the side, it wasn't long before Billy Bonds was getting mentions in the papers.

10

I still have a cutting in which Sam Bartram, who I could just about remember in Charlton's goal, declared he would 'eat his hat if this kid Bonds does not play for England'. Well, as things turned out, I never did. I don't suppose the late Sam ever ate his headgear, either! But it was encouraging for a young player to read such flattering comments.

They were soon followed by suggestions that various top clubs were having a look, too. Colin Appleton, who'd played for Leicester in the Cup final, was with us then, and one day he told me he'd heard a whisper that Southampton were coming in with an offer. Sunderland and Leicester were other clubs supposed to be interested. But I was never one for knocking on the manager's door and asking what it was all about every time such reports appeared in the papers. I trusted Bob Stokoe and felt he would be honest if there was any chance of me making a good move. I was also very much a Londoner and, frankly, the idea of leaving the capital for somewhere like Roker did not much interest me. I suppose I would have gone north if nothing else had turned up. But soon something did.

It came the day after Charlton had lost to West Ham in the semi-final of the Wembley fives one Wednesday night in April. Bob called me into his office the next day and said Ron Greenwood wanted to talk to me, and was I interested? Of course I was! We'd been unlucky to lose that fives semi to the Hammers, who went on to beat Arsenal for the trophy. They beat us 2–1, but only with a really sloppy goal.

The game sticks in my memory because of the fuss Budgie Byrne kicked up all through it. He really seemed to have the wind up when they looked like losing. We found out later Budgie had got ten to one odds on them winning the tournament! How he ever managed that I cannot imagine, because West Ham had an impressive side out – Colin Mackleworth in goal, plus

Mooro, Martin Peters, Geoff Hurst, Johnny Byrne and John Sissons as sub.

When I was his team-mate later I learned that, after that night, Hurstie told his manager: 'If you are looking for a right-back, what about this Billy Bonds?' I don't suppose that made any difference to Ron Greenwood's views about me ... but it can't have hurt, either.

Anyway, West Ham's boss turned up at The Valley two days later. We were playing our final match of the season against Birmingham and he watched us win by the only goal before meeting me.

But I put my big foot in it straight away with him. Bob left us alone in his office and Ron told me what the deal would mean and why he wanted me. All I needed to say was 'Yes, please.' But I somehow had the idea it would not do to seem too keen and started mumbling something about other clubs being interested as well.

Ron did not say a word; just got up from his chair and walked out. I sat there wondering if I'd blown it, and then Bob Stokoe stormed in, red-faced, and fixed me with those gimlet eyes. 'What the hell do you think you are up to? You agree to meet Ron Greenwood and then start talking about other clubs. Are you barmy?'

That was the end of my negotiating position. Ron returned and, in a very short time, everything was settled – with nobody mentioning the little upset!

The next day Bob took me in his car – I still only had a bike – over to Upton Park to watch West Ham finish their season with a 1–1 draw against Manchester City. My actual signing on the dotted line was to be done after that game.

Bob and I were shown into Ron Greenwood's office and had to wait a little while before he joined us. I remember Bob gazing round at the plush carpet, wood panelling, ultra modern desk and everything, and then commenting: 'You know, Billy, one day I am going to be manager at a club like this.'

That remark put the whole situation into perspective for me. For several years my sole aim had been to win and hold a first team spot with Charlton. That was the only ambition, the limit of my horizons. Throughout that time the manager's word was law and everything he said aimed at seeking success for Charlton. But now I was leaving he could openly talk in a way that showed that for him, just as much as me, Charlton Athletic was not the final pinnacle.

When Ron Greenwood joined us, however, it quickly seemed once again that the transfer would be off. He called in two of his players, Denis Burnett and Trevor Dawkins, and told them the idea was for an exchange deal, with them moving to Charlton.

Of course, I had no inkling of anything which might have been going on between the pair and him, and I was aghast when, almost in unison, they replied, 'No thanks', and just walked out without another word!

My face must have fallen a mile. But I later suspected that answer was exactly what Ron anticipated, and that he merely went through the motions so Bob Stokoe would hear it from the horse's mouth. Because he just grinned at me and said: 'There's no problem, Billy, we'll just pay cash.' The fee was agreed at £48,500, with another couple of thousand thrown in if I played for England.

What a relief to hear that! No doubt, the two managers had already done all the talking on the phone beforehand, but, raw as I was, I did not appreciate that. Suddenly I was a rich man! The thirty quid a week I was on at Charlton was doubled, and I also got a signing-on payment equal to five per cent of the transfer fee.

When Bob and I got back to Charlton in his car later that night I was still trying to work out in my head what five per cent of £48,500 was ... wishing I'd done better at maths while at school. But one thing I knew for sure: Billy Bonds had more dough than ever before in his life!

11

Though it was the end of the season, my debut for West Ham came only two days later. And a real spectre-at-the-wedding feast performance it turned out!

I signed on the dotted line that Saturday evening and was back at Upton Park the following Monday night to play for Hammers in Ken Brown's testimonial match. With Brownie the crowd's favourite, it was a light-hearted affair, and the whole ground had a carnival atmosphere. Which did not suit me one bit. I wanted to get out there and show them what Billy Bonds was all about, make a few tackles and get stuck in.

But it wasn't the night for that. I remember Peter Brabrook shaping up to take a corner kick and having the crowd in fits by kicking the corner flag instead of the ball. He also had them chuckling – at my expense – when he made as if to put a throw-in to my feet but then let the ball slip back over his head. I trapped a non-existent ball, which everyone thought was hilarious.

I was glad to get off and stay off at half-time, fortunately with the valid excuse of trouble from a soft corn between my toes.

Back at Charlton the transfer had caused something of a rumpus among Valley fans, who sent angry letters to the local press and to the club about my going. I understood their feelings. Nothing is more galling for true-blue supporters than to watch a kid develop through their club's ranks and then be sold. But equally you can't fault a player for accepting a move that's to his benefit, as was mine to West Ham.

That's the one big difference between being a supporter and being a player. For supporters the club is their life, a habit that's in the blood. Players have loyalty, too, but for them it is still a job of work and, as with any other job, situations arise that it would be silly to ignore.

It's happened to West Ham often enough – Paul Allen's transfer to Spurs an outstanding recent example. Nobody was more sorry than me to see Ollie leave. In many ways he reminded me of myself at his age. Right from his earliest days with the club, Ollie put everything into it, working just as hard in training as he did in games. In fact, you always had to watch yourself if you happened to go in a bit hard on him in fives – because he made quite sure you got it back! With that kind of passion, emotion is not far below the surface, and I wasn't surprised when, after he became the youngest player ever to earn an FA Cup winner's medal when we beat Arsenal, Ollie's face streamed tears on the Wembley pitch. But when he later decided to move I sincerely wished him all the best, just as my Charlton club-mates had when I left.

Mind you, I also warned him to watch out whenever Spurs met us!

12

I got an early taste of the big time with West Ham, because they had an end-of-season trip to Ireland arranged to play Shamrock Rovers. The only such jaunt I'd had with Charlton had been a week in Holland for a youth tournament some years earlier. We'd gone over by boat and stayed with Dutch families. With Hammers to Ireland it was first-class all the way, flying there and staying in the best hotel. I think the game ended in a 5–5 frolic.

The man I saw most at West Ham at that time was Rob Jenkins, who had taken over as club physio following the death of his Dad, Bill. The broken nose I'd got at Portsmouth was still troublesome, making it very difficult for me to breathe properly. Rob it was who arranged for me to enter hospital during the close season for an operation to put it right – and again it was all top-class treatment, with a private room and everything.

The surgeon who operated gave me two options. 'I can do a cosmetic job and give you a neat little nose. But if I do, the first real whack you get will spread it all over your face again. Or I can leave you with the kind of nose you already have which will stand up to any rough treatment,' he announced. Playing the way I did, he had no real reason to ask which I wanted! Everything was in good working order by the time I reported back for my first pre-season training with West Ham.

Ron Greenwood was a great admirer of Continental football and had organised a pre-season tour to Finland, Switzerland and Germany. With what I learned was his usual thoroughness, Ron planned the trip as a steady build-up, so that the games became increasingly hard and we finished with the toughest just before starting our own season.

The opener, against HJK in Helsinki, we won 6–3. We moved from there to Switzerland, where we beat Lugano and then Grasshoppers. The latter game, in Zurich, was notable for the first-team debut of Trevor Brooking.

The final tour match took us to Borussia Dortmund, one of Germany's top sides at the time. And it brought us down to earth after those three much easier games . . . because they gave us a real lesson with a 4–1 hiding. But it was not as bad as it looks, since the Germans were about three weeks ahead of us in their own pre-season work.

We returned to start the new season with a home game against Sheffield Wednesday – and a line-up including two other newcomers besides me: goalkeeper Bobby 'Fester' Ferguson and centre-half John Cushley.

Fester had cost a British record £65,000 from Kilmarnock, where he'd won regular Scotland caps. Fellow-Scot Cush came from Celtic for £25,000, and had the job of taking over from the departed Ken Brown.

It had all the signs of being a winning start, with goals from Geoff Hurst and Martin Peters putting us 2–1 ahead. But Wednesday got two late replies to beat us 3–2 – their winner from Jim McCalliog the kind of header you would not expect to get past a goalkeeper who cost so much!

We were at home again the next Monday and, after some fumbling, beat Burnley 4–2. But then we went to Spurs and got hammered 5–1 in front of a crowd of over 55,000.

In those days the programme was arranged so you met one club twice very early in the season, and after the White Hart Lane disaster, we went to Burnley. Trevor Brooking made his League debut and we took a 3–3 draw. Defeats at home to Manchester United and away to Everton followed before we won 5–1 at Roker Park. This triumph was marred by a home reverse against Wolves in our next outing, but a win at Fulham and home draw with Leeds underlined just how inconsistent West Ham were . . . and would be for so many years.

Not long after, in fact, we achieved the singular feat of losing 4–3 at home to Stoke . . . after being three up!

How can anyone do that, you wonder now? Well, that was West Ham in those days – always the great entertainers – and 30,000 would turn up to watch in anticipation of seeing something a bit special. I was talking about those attendances – with Hammers in the bottom six – not long back, and Phil Parkes quietly pointed out that it was twenty years ago. That's the trouble with having been about for so long!

While the West Ham philosophy often made for spectacular games, it was never going to win the League. The Liverpools and Leeds would never let anyone off the hook the way we would. If they got three up, they simply closed the game down, waited for the opposition to push forward, and then nicked a couple more on the break to wrap it up. But as in that Stoke affair, Hammers could not play that way. Three up, all they wanted was to steam ahead all over the place and get another three. Doing that created space at the back for the opposition to exploit, which Stoke did to such effect on the day.

It's not on now. A mere two decades later and results are so all-important that no team would dream of taking such risks, nor would any manager let them.

I may be wrong, but there could well be a link between present attitudes in the game and the smaller crowds everyone pulls in. For my first League game at West Ham it was almost 30,000, while at Spurs the following week it was nearly double that number.

So where have they all gone? There's no doubt that football now is all about work-rate and organisation, to the detriment of individual flair. But those qualities are counter-productive in the end. Goals are what the paying customer wants to see. If there are fewer of those, there will be fewer spectators.

13

The year I moved to West Ham, 1967, proved of lifelong significance for me, apart from football. Just after we came back from that pre-season Continental tour I met for the first time the girl who was to become my wife.

With a couple of friends, I dropped in one night at a small dance in Downham. The lads I was with knew some girls who were also there. One was named Lyn, and she and I soon found we got along very well, discovering similar interests and enthusiasms outside our work. Lyn was employed in a City office, and I suppose I must, at some stage in that first evening, have told her I was a footballer and had just joined West Ham. If I did, it could have made very little impact. Lyn had never been to a game in her life, and certainly was not impressed at meeting a footballer.

Which was perhaps just as well for me. Some girls would probably have had reservations about getting involved with a guy whose business they might regard as either glamorous or a bit 'iffy'. They might also think to themselves: 'Oh, yes – tell me another', hearing someone they'd just met at a dance claiming he played football for a big pro club! It was also a good thing neither of us are that superstitious, because the day in question happened to be August 13.

We were engaged ten months later, on Lyn's eighteenth birthday, and after another two years we got married.

Neither of us can recall now just when Lyn first came to a match to watch her future husband at work.

She eventually began going with my parents, and later her own mum became a regular and keen companion at games with her. But not her dad – he was, and is, a lifelong Millwall supporter and, as their home games clashed with ours, the only time he went to Upton Park was for evening matches.

For my first two or three West Ham home games after joining the club I either got a lift to the ground in someone's car or else made my own way on public transport. For someone with no West Ham background, sitting on a bus crowded with fans bound for Upton Park was an interesting, and useful, experience. I'd not been a Hammer long enough for anyone to recognise me, and I usually sat, with my nose stuck in a book or paper, ear-wigging all the comments. They told me a lot about how West Ham supporters felt about their club – and I admit I was tickled pink when someone commented: 'This new bloke Bond looks a bit useful', even if they hadn't got the name quite right! After having John Bond at number two for so many years, I suppose it was inevitable that it would take Hammers followers some time before they put the S on the end for me.

In some quarters it has been the done thing to dismiss supporters' knowledge and understanding of the game. But not with me. The pros must know more, otherwise they would not be in the job. But the chap on the terrace, apart from paying our wages, is not the mug many seem to think when it comes to having valid opinions about football. I found this out at Charlton when I sometimes slipped in at the back of the Kop terrace to watch a first team game. Nobody around me knew I was on the Valley staff, so I looked and listened 'incognito' – and more often than not found I agreed wholeheartedly with the views expressed, if not perhaps the manner.

Really, it all goes back to what Jock Basford used to preach. Football is a simple game. To try, as some do, to give it a mystique, the secrets of which are known only to a select few, is merely an attempt to feel superior.

The man who took me to West Ham, Ron Greenwood, acquired something of a reputation for this, but nothing could be more wrong. In my considerable experience, Ron never deliberately set out to look down on either players or fans. But what he did demand was for thought to be given to the game. Physical weaknesses or deficiencies in skill he would accept, but never a failure to work hard mentally, and he had little time for anyone he suspected could not be bothered to do this.

I like to feel I have always thought about football, listening to every bit of advice and trying to improve all the time. My basic philosophy as a full-back, however, was simply to force my winger to go back the other way. If I kept him fully occupied trying to stop me going forward, then he was not able to do his primary attacking job. So my development into an 'attacking' defender was largely because, in my view, it was the best way of defending ... and I wouldn't mind a quid for every time Ron Greenwood told us just that!

14

Ron Greenwood was in marked contrast to my previous boss, Bob Stokoe. John Lyall, Hammers' present chief, has a bit of both men in his approach as a manager. I count myself lucky to have worked under such a trio.

Bob was full of passion. He got a response from his player through a sheer 'death or glory' emotional appeal. 'Get out there, get your foot in, win the ball – and then think about playing' was Bob's philosophy, very much the way he played as a staunch centre-half.

There was plenty of emotion about Ron, but he kept it well below the surface under tight control. Only occasionally did his guard drop so that you saw the feelings underneath. Ron had a reputation for being distant and aloof, but there are many in football who benefited from his generosity and who would not be where they are today but for his influence upon them.

Nobody ever thought more deeply about the game. Ron will happily spend hours talking football, but he does not suffer fools gladly – and players who don't think about their business come into that category for him. His dismissive attitude to such people is largely, I suspect, the reason he is sometimes regarded as unapproachable. 'A lively mind means a lively body' was one of his constant themes. It's perhaps a fairly trite saying, but a true one all the same.

I owe a great deal to both Bob and Ron. At Charlton Bob's influence set me firmly on the right path, adding a little bit of steel to my already energetic style. He made me understand that, as a defender, my first job was to let the winger know I was there.

Bob impressed on us the importance of what happened early on, how it could often have a significant bearing on the whole game. 'The earlier your first contact with the opposition the better. Give him a taste of what you are about, let him know what to expect when he tries to go past you again,' he said.

A hard man on and off the field, Bob still always made the distinction between being tough and playing dirty. That first, vital contact had to be within the laws, otherwise it was worse than none at all, in his view. If you had to foul an opponent to stop him, it merely handed him the psychological advantage you were trying to establish for yourself.

There were plenty of rough edges to my game when I joined Hammers – don't get me wrong, I know there still are! But many were smoothed out by the influence of Ron Greenwood and, later, John Lyall.

Ron really opened my mind about football. He talked about aspects that had never before entered my head, like diversionary running, supporting play, the creation and use of space, the denial of it to the opposition. There was also far more actual ball work in his training schedules than I ever did at Charlton.

That probably stemmed from Ron's own experiences as a player in the early post-war years. Some clubs then had the quaint idea that if players were not allowed to see a ball during the week they would want it more on Saturdays! For a man with Ron's perceptions it must have been sheer hell. Obviously, if you lack a good enough touch there wasn't much point in getting possession, and the only way ball skills are improved is by constant work with a ball.

It was a tragedy – for both Ron and England – that he did not immediately follow Alf Ramsey as national manager. The people who gave the job to Don Revie doubtless had their very good reasons. But it should have gone to Ron.

England manager was his proper level. With players of international ability, Ron did not need to waste his energies upon the motivation that is necessary in the bread-and-butter stuff of club competition. Motivation was definitely not one of his strengths as a manager. When he took over with England he worked with a squad of the best players who needed no gee-up. He could concentrate upon tactics – collective and individual – and at that he is the best.

Hammers learned this playing in Europe. Ron's assessment of the opposition was always spot-on. When the action started you felt as if you'd been playing them for years instead of for the first time.

So why, with such an excellent manager and three of England's 1966 World Cup-winning side, did West Ham not achieve more? Perhaps part of the answer is that Ron was, at times, too much of an intellectual. He wanted all his players to be fully involved in team talks, tried to get a feed-back from the whole squad, with everyone chipping in their two-penn'orth. But not all players find it easy to talk football, however well they can play it. There was also a constant risk about putting your oar in at those team meetings. Very often Ron seemed to turn your opinion into an argument, demolished what you said – and left you wishing you'd kept quiet!

Which, in the end, is what a lot did.

15

The one big disappointment of my career has to be missing out on a full England cap, which I would have loved for my dad's sake rather than my own. When Ron Greenwood became England's chief he included me three times in his squads – only on one occasion did I actually pull on that shirt, when I was sub against Italy. After winning two Young England caps in Alf Ramsey's time, I had every hope I would progress to the full England team, particularly when I was in my mid-twenties and, in my view, playing at a personal peak.

I thought the breakthrough had arrived one day when Ron Greenwood called me into his office at Upton Park and told me he'd been on the phone to Alf. 'I told Alf how very well you are playing at the moment, and that if he wants an attacking defender he could do no better than you,' he said. But almost before the hope flashed into my mind that I was to get a call-up, Ron added: 'Trouble is, William, Alf says he does not like the way you run. He reckons there's something ungainly in your gait.'

Ron was obviously disconcerted by the England manager's opinion of his West Ham defender ... but not half as much as I was! If the man in charge of England was thinking like that, it was pretty obvious I could forget about playing at that level while he was around. It was a real choker for me. There were other criticisms that could have been made of me which I would have found acceptable, but to be written off because of the way I ran seemed almost laughable.

Club-mates like Bobby Moore and Trevor Brooking were both notably stylish operators. Yet I wouldn't like to think they got their international chances just because they looked good on the ball. And with all due respect to a player I always admired immensely, Nobby Stiles was hardly the most elegant in action – but he was one of the stars of the Ramsey side which won the World Cup.

I left Ron's office a bit disappointed. For years I had believed that judgement of a player related solely to how effectively he did his particular job. Both Bob Stokoe and Ron Greenwood had improved my game by pointing out certain aspects of it which I could improve. Neither at any time had ever passed comment upon the way I moved.

The worst of it was that I had always regarded myself as a 'natural' runner, over any distance, and took great pride in the fact. Many players find the routine running in training a boring drag. I never have. Even during the close season I always go out at least a couple of nights a week putting in the mileage.

Ron's subsequent inclusion of me in three of his England squads showed he, at least, had no reservations about my style of running. But the nearest I finally ever came to a full cap was being on the bench at Wembley for a vital World Cup qualifier against the Italians. Their press were certain before the game that I would be playing. 'England pick Bonds to do marking job' was the line they took. In fact, I sat out the entire game as one of the subs while England made certain of reaching the finals with a 2–0 win.

My friends have never forgiven Ron Greenwood for not putting me on for the last few minutes. 'After being your manager at West Ham for so long, he could at least have made sure you got one cap,' they moaned.

But they don't understand Ron. His job that night was to ensure England won and went to Argentina ... not to do Billy Bonds a favour, however long we had worked together previously. If the match had been a mere warm-up friendly somewhere, then I am certain Ron would have had me off the bench to earn that one cap. With 100,000 fans urging England on to beat an Italian side full of fine players that particular night, however, he was not about to take the slightest risk. Funny things can happen in football, as we all know, and a two goal lead vanish in seconds against that kind of opposition. So I never had any complaints. I was just delighted to be involved with England.

Ron never said anything about why he had not played me, as the Italians so obviously anticipated he would. It might just have had something to do with the previous Saturday, when

Ron watched West Ham play West Brom at Upton Park. I had easily the worst game of my entire career! To this day I can't explain why. After playing under Ron for so many years he knew everything about me, so there was absolutely no need for me to try and impress. But I found myself doing things all through the game that were completely out of character.

Leading Albion's attack was David Cross, who later became a great West Ham team-mate. At one point in the match I found myself back-marker in defence with the ball at my feet and nobody else between me and our goal. Crossie moved in to close me down and, of all things, I tried to take the ball round him ... a repeat of that elementary clanger against Plymouth so many years before! He nicked it off me and only a good Mervyn Day save rescued me.

Perhaps my nightmare game influenced Ron when he picked his England side for the following Wednesday's game. I doubt it, though. But whatever there may be in that, Ron soon showed I was very much in his England thinking by naming me for a later friendly in West Germany. On the Saturday before that mid-week trip, however, I copped a knock playing for Hammers at Everton and had to pull out.

I think it upset Ron almost as much as me, because when Brazil came to Wembley later on he took the trouble to phone personally and tell me I was definitely going to play, not just be in the squad.

It was the game in which my West Ham team-mate Alvin Martin was to make his England debut. 'It will be great for the pair of you to be playing together for England,' said Ron.

The Brazil match was also mid-week and the previous Friday West Ham played Sheffield Wednesday in a League match. Wednesday are always hard opposition, with an impressive work-rate and total commitment, so it was the kind of encounter in which you might well take a knock or two.

But the one I collected came from a team-mate, our goalkeeper Phil Parkes! Big 'Eric', as we call him, came hurtling out of goal like an express train, too fast for me to get out of his way, and I stopped all $15\frac{1}{2}$ stones of him, taking the worst impact in my side.

I knew immediately it had done some real damage, although

I played out the rest of the game. I gave it the Saturday to see if the injury would ease out, but on the Sunday morning I was still very sore around the chest and side. I shoved on a track suit and trainers and went straight away to a local cricket ground just down the road from our house. One run across that confirmed my fears. I couldn't breath deeply without a sharp pain in my side.

Fed right up, I walked back home and phoned the England team's hotel. Ron had just arrived and I had to tell him: 'I think I've busted my ribs.' 'That's unfortunate – are you sure you can't make it?' he asked. But Ron knew the answer. Many a time he'd seen me go out and play patched up and padded . . . and if I said myself I was unfit, then I was!

Nobody was more upset than Phil when he learned our collision had cost me a cap. He was genuinely miserable because, having played just once himself for England, he knew how important to a player achieving that milestone is.

But he was in no way to blame. If he had not gone for the ball and Wednesday had scored, then Phil would have got a deserved rucking after the game. It was down to me to get out of his way . . . and after that I made sure I always did. 'Just make sure you shout nice and loud when you're coming out, Phil,' I told him. Now when I hear that 'My ball' roar from behind me I'm off sprinting like mad for the edge of the area – well out of big Eric's path!

The Brazil game was the last time I got near a cap. I still feel fate was against it all along.

I am not a particularly superstitious type, but it's often hard not to think some things are indeed written in the stars. For instance, you often hear it said 'If your name is on the Cup . . .' I bet no side yet has ever taken the trophy away from Wembley without also thinking back to the several heart-stopping moments along the way when it could all so easily have gone wrong. Twice I've been lucky enough to be on the winning side there. Both times the experiences en route convinced us West Ham's name was on the Cup right from the start!

16

Holding the FA Cup up above my head in front of a claret-and-blue sea at Wembley in 1975 was easily the high spot of my career to that point. But I was seriously worried that it might also be my swan-song.

It's the dream of every captain to lead his side to triumph in the Cup final. A great many fine players have never experienced that unforgettable moment when the trophy is actually placed in your hands, and you turn to face a ground black with jubilant fans, raise the Cup aloft and then feel the shock waves from the roar that goes up.

At that precise moment you lose touch with reality. Cloud nine becomes a fact. For your team-mates and you the world has never been better. It is a feeling that can never be taken away from you.

Yet that whole Cup campaign was not one I could say I really enjoyed. From the start of the season I was plagued with groin trouble. Despite intensive treatment and periods of resting, the problem became progressively worse, until I was missing out on League games and getting through cup ties only with cortisone injections and tablets. I knew in my heart it was something that only surgery would clear up, if it could be done at all. But there was no way this could be tried before the next close season.

Our route to the final started at The Dell, where we beat a very useful Southampton side 2–1 in the third round. It was a hard encounter, a typical cup clash, with full-blooded tackles flying about. I remember that after the game Saints' Peter Osgood came looking for Bobby Gould. Bobby and I came out of the visitors' dressing-room – and there was Ossie waiting to have words about something our striker had done during the game. Ossie was a big old lad and, while hardly the most retiring of men himself, Gouldie wisely bottled it and beat a quick retreat with me. Definitely a situation where discretion was the better part of valour!

The next round favoured us with a home draw against Third Division Swindon. It was an omen to some, because they were among Hammers' victims in the club's first-ever Cup final success in 1964. But others remembered that the Wiltshire club made headlines by taking a 3–3 draw at Upton Park in the 1967 third round, and then winning the replay 3–1.

That was the season before I joined West Ham. Swindon were pushing hard for promotion to Division Two when they came back in 1975. Billy Jennings gave us the lead fifteen minutes from time, but the scene was all set for a repeat of history when Peter Eastoe equalised with eight minutes left to take us back for a County Ground replay.

The press certainly anticipated another giant-killing act and turned up in force the following Tuesday night.

On a terrible, glue-pot pitch Peter Anderson gave Swindon a half-time lead. But Trevor Brooking equalised – a header, too – and five minutes from the finish, with extra-time looming, Patsy Holland had the reporters furiously tearing up their stories with our winner.

In the next round we were again at home, to a QPR side with Phil Parkes in goal. We had won 2–0 in the League at Rangers the previous November, but they had improved immensely since then and, having drawn 2–2 in the Upton Park return only a month earlier, were hot favourites to go on in the Cup. Dave Clement put them in front, but Patsy Holland quickly equalised and Keith Robson's goal in the first minute after the interval proved the winner of a tremendous game, watched by close on 40,000. So it was West Ham who went to Highbury to face Arsenal in the quarter-finals.

Home advantage made the Gunners the tip to reach the last four in most quarters. On a wet, skiddy top, however, our 'secret weapon' turned out to be the virtually unknown Alan Taylor, who got both goals in a 2–0 win ... the start for him of an incredible 'Roy of the Rovers' story.

Ron Greenwood had paid Rochdale £40,000 a few months before to take Alan out of the obscurity of the Fourth Division. Before that Highbury tie he had not even started a first team game. A smashing north country lad, Alan was immediately dubbed 'Sparrer' by the rest of us because of his frail physique and painfully thin, match-stick limbs. But he could motor.

Whether or not Arsenal had not done their home-work properly, I can't say. They certainly did not seem prepared for Sparrer's pace, though. I remember one of our goals came from someone simply sticking the ball inside Bob McNab, who was left for dead as Sparrer streaked by to beat Jimmy Rimmer.

Yet we left Highbury feeling even more strongly that our name was on the Cup. For the tie really turned upon another incident. John Radford was put clean through and brought crashing down by Mervyn Day's rush out of goal. It looked a penalty to me – and Arsenal were convinced to a man it was. But the man in charge, Ken Burns, among the day's top refs, ruled the foul was inches outside the area, and we scrambled the free-kick away.

Two seasons later Raddy became a Hammer ... and almost the first thing he did was to go on about the penalty we got away with in that cup tie!

By then I was West Ham skipper, Bobby Moore having departed to Fulham the previous season. When we were two up at Highbury, with the semi-finals beckoning, I did my job as captain by urging everyone to stick at it and keep the game tight. My opposite number was Alan Ball and, well before the finish, Ballie said sadly to me: 'I shouldn't bother with all that shouting, Bonzo, we're never going to win today.' He was right – but his advice only made me yell all the more!

Because of my groin problem I had missed the two previous League games; but I returned for the next one after the Arsenal win, against Burnley at Upton Park. At Turf Moor much earlier in the season we won 5–3, and I was among our scorers. But the return encounter proved a personal disaster. We won 2–1, with Sparrer bagging his first League goal. I did not see the finish, however, because I was already at hospital having a really bad cut stitched. I copped the injury almost as soon as the game started, challenging Burnley's Peter Noble with a sliding tackle. As I went in, leg fully stretched, Peter wisely leaped over me. One of his studs ripped right across my knee-cap, the nylon opening up a very nasty gash.

A radio commentator at the match declared the cut needed a sewing-machine. Lyn was at home and, hearing those horrific words, was in a right old state by the time I arrived that evening, with my knee heavily bandaged. But worries of that kind are all part of being a footballer's wife, I'm afraid.

Yet if the hospital did not quite require that sewing-machine, the injury was serious enough to put in jeopardy my chances of playing the Cup semi-finals, which were less than a month away. The cut across the knee-cap was in the worst possible place, with the constant risk of opening it up again every time I bent my leg. With the persistent groin trouble as well, it was a particularly gloomy time for me.

There were several visits to West Ham's club specialist Brian Roper about the groin, and these only confirmed that an operation was necessary. Success in such matters can never be guaranteed, and for the first time I suddenly realised I could be facing the end of the road as a player. I'd always, I suppose, accepted that I would pack in around 32 or 33, at least as a Division One player, but that was still some way off and I'd never even thought beyond it. 'What the hell will I do if I'm finished?' I wondered.

Lyn was a tremendous support in this unexpected situation. Going home together in our car from seeing Brian Roper we would talk about what kind of future we could expect if I had to quit, what it would mean financially, what I might find for a job.

It was an unnerving position to suddenly confront. No doubt, Lyn was every bit as anxious as me, especially as by then we had a young daughter. But she did not let it show and was full of optimism that things would work out fine, whatever happened. It doesn't sound much, put in those few words, but her down-to-earth support was invaluable to me.

Fortunately, I've always been a good healer and that cut proved no exception. Even so, my training was severely restricted and I could really only do weights and stomachs.

I did not play again until we went to Villa Park to face Ipswich in the semi-final. As a spectacle it was a non-event. Both sides concentrated upon not losing rather than winning, there were very few chances at either end, and I think all the players involved were heartily glad when it ended 0–0 and we all had another chance.

The replay was staged midweek at Stamford Bridge, with snow falling. Sparrer bagged another brace and we won 2–1. But to this day Ipswich remain convinced they were the better side on the night, being particularly incensed when they had a goal ruled off-side. Clive Thomas was the ref and he gave somebody other than the scorer off-side as the ball went in. It was a decision by the controversial Welsh official which several of the Hammers afield that cold night would have cause to remember some years later on another very important occasion!

The other semi-final also went to a replay before Fulham beat Birmingham – one of three First Division scalps the Division Two Cottagers collected on their way to a shock Wembley appearance.

The London derby final meant West Ham meeting as an opponent our old idol Bobby Moore, who had moved across London the previous season. Along with another former England man, Alan Mullery, Bobby had typically proved utterly wrong those who had been only too ready to write him off.

As in the 1964 final, Division One Hammers again faced Second Division opposition and, once more, were very much expected winners. The outcome was a predictable 2–0 West Ham win in a game that never touched memorable heights. Carrying the groin problem, I did not enjoy it as much as I would have liked to, being aware all through the game that I was not able to play to my full capacity.

But the match completed Sparrer's amazing, meteoric climb from Division Four to Cup final hero, because he once again netted both goals, giving him the rare distinction of scoring twice in quarter-final, semi-final and final.

We were not to know it at the time, but that was the peak of his career. Sparrer was never again to hit such consistency, and one can now see it as the kind of 'golden' spell some players briefly enjoy, when everything they touch around goal goes right.

In 1973–74, for instance, I had just that kind of season. Playing in midfield, I finished as Hammers' leading League scorer with thirteen goals, one more than the big man, Clyde Best. At one point I bagged seven in five games, including my only hat-trick when we beat Chelsea 3–0 at Upton Park. I should have had another one two matches later. We lost 3–2 at home to Coventry. I got both goals ... and also missed the easiest chance to come my way all season! With that sort of run not even the player himself can really say why it is going so well. You certainly are not working any harder, but somehow every time you get a sniff of goal it comes off.

One of the thirteen I got that season was reported as a fine glancing header. That's what I meant it to be but, in fact, I got my timing all wrong, missed contact completely with my forehead, and the ball flew in off my lug-hole. My ear was still ringing as I ran back to the centre, with all the lads around me shouting 'Great header, Bonzo!'

Similarly, one of Alan's Cup final goals came when Fulham's goalkeeper Peter Mellor fielded a low cross into the box and then dropped it right at his feet. All credit to Sparrer for following in for just that possibility, but he could do it ninety-nine times in a hundred without getting that gift, particularly in the Cup final. But what he achieved in those few months is there for all time in the records. They talk about the romance of the Cup. There was surely never a more classic example!

17

When West Ham went back to Wembley five years later it was a somewhat uneven campaign for me, even though I played at times as satisfyingly as at any time in my career.

That I was still playing at all was down entirely to one man, Brian Roper, Hammers' consultant specialist, whose surgical skills have twice given me a new lease of active life.

Immediately after the 1975 final Brian had me in hospital for the 'make or break' operation on the groin injury which had dogged me all the season and was a serious threat to my career. What Brian did technically I don't know, but it was a very complex job and meant virtually replacing a joint.

I hate being in hospital, so I was back home about four or five days after the op and spent the close season sunning myself in the garden.

Thanks to Brian Roper's ability, the operation was successful. But it remained to be seen if I could ever be the same player again. Nobody ever actually hinted at this to me, but I remember thinking that it must be in everyone's mind. Bonzo was a bit too long in the tooth to ever really come back from surgery of that kind.

The 1975–76 season began for West Ham, as Cup winners, at Wembley, with the Charity Shield pre-season game against the champions Derby. Still convalescing, I was not there, and I listened to us on the radio losing 2–0 as I lay soaking up the sun at home in the garden.

By the time we started on the 1979–80 cup trail, however, I was well back in action, striving to lead Hammers back to the First Division from which they had slipped two seasons earlier.

Despite that fall from grace, we simply did not ever really accept ourselves as a Second Division side, even though we had not bounced back immediately to the top flight as many had expected. With players like Trevor Brooking, Alan Devonshire, Alvin Martin, Ray Stewart and Paul Allen, we considered the side a match for most Division One teams.

This feeling was put to the test in our first FA Cup game that season when we were drawn away to First Division Albion. Stuart Pearson gave us a first-half lead – but after that it was Phil Parkes versus Albion. Big Eric's display that day I still regard as the finest I've seen. I can see now the world-class saves he made from big Regis and Gary Owen. During the interval Phil and I found ourselves next to each other in the toilet and I told him: 'Phil, after what you've stopped so far West Ham's name could be on the Cup this year.' Both of us recalled that little prophecy later.

Albion boss Ron Atkinson reckoned afterwards that Phil deserved 12 marks out of 10. Certainly, it was only down to him that we earned a replay. We almost avoided that, too, because Albion's equaliser by Regis came with less than a minute left.

The tie was a no-quarter affair, both sides giving as good as they got. But Albion's chairman Bert Millichip was badly upset afterwards because I'd pulled back Regis at one point, and he told West Ham officials his opinion of the incident. I dismissed the matter from my mind at the time. But it was to return with a vengeance later that season!

Injury sidelined me for the Upton Park replay with Albion, which West Ham won 2–1. The margin did not reflect play, and for much of the night the biggest worry was that increasingly dense mist might force the game to be called off.

Albion's Ally Brown scored their goal four minutes from the finish, just after Trevor had added to the lead Pikey had given us. But though the final moments were then a bit tense, Albion could have no complaints ... only regrets that they had not managed to beat Phil more than once at The Hawthorns.

The fourth round gave us a short away trip to our East London neighbours, Second Division Orient.

Barely three weeks before, we'd gone there in the League and won 4–0, so we went back full of confidence. But we also knew it would not be quite so easy this time. The League game on New Year's Day was played on a frozen top for which we were well equipped with boots specially designed for such conditions.

While Orient skidded and slid we had few problems keeping our feet.

Playing the Os then was a real 'old boys' job. Their manager Jimmy Bloomfield was an ex-Hammer, and they also had Mervyn Day, Tommy Taylor and Billy Jennings, all of whom helped West Ham win the Cup in 1975.

The injury which kept me out of the Albion replay had mended – but another one followed to threaten my chances of facing Orient. It happened in a home League game against Preston the week before the cup tie. A high ball was knocked over my head, I turned to get it . . . and suddenly the sky went dark. Alvin had decided it was his ball, not mine, went for a full-blooded clearance, and all I saw was his enormous size eleven boot blotting out everything before it hit me full in the face.

There was blood everywhere. I wasn't unconscious, and I remember thinking: 'A bit lower and the old hooter would have gone again.' I was not sure it hadn't as Rob Jenkins helped me off, with blood-soaked pads over my face. The damage proved to be two nasty cuts, one almost vertical down my forehead and the other under an eyebrow just above my eyelid.

Take my advice, getting out of the way of Stretch comes second only to avoiding Parkesie!

With only a week to go it looked very much as if I would be watching – out of one eye – rather than playing at Orient. Rob came to the rescue, devising padding to protect the stitched-up wounds, held in place with plaster and heavy bandaging. Though I looked like a case for intensive care, I felt it would work.

Before the match Rob went with me to the ref's room to get his agreement that it was all right for me to play sporting this imposing headgear. He passed it – but his look suggested he felt I was barmy.

And, of course, it had to be Tommy Taylor I went to the centre with for the toss-up!

Tommy is one of life's jokers, getting a laugh out of everyone and everything. After being his team-mate at West Ham for so long, I guessed he would be up to his usual tricks. I wasn't wrong. Tommy trotted up wearing a funny hat and false nose.

It wasn't long after Christmas and I expect he got them out of a cracker. He took one look at my bandaged bonce and, with a raised palm, said solemnly: 'How, Geronimo!'

The ref, Bristol's S.G. Bates, must have been firmly convinced by then that *everyone* in the game was crackers. But he and his linesmen had a good chuckle.

It was one time, however, when I at any rate was not prepared to join in Tom's bit of fun. Psyched-up for the game, I just wanted to get on with the serious business, not lark about and have my concentration disrupted.

Tommy was soon laughing even more after putting the Os ahead from the spot, following a penalty I gave away.

The bandage was the real culprit. Swathed round my head, it impaired the vision in one eye so I had to look down my nose, the way a soldier in a busby seems to. Because of this, I did not get an early sight of the ball, reacted late, and conceded the penalty.

After that, I kept shoving the bandage up as best I could but it remained a problem for the whole game. Fortunately, an own goal and a Tonka penalty put us ahead by the break and, though John Chiedozie equalised, Ray fired a late winner.

Afterwards I resisted the strong temptation to find Tom and tell him: 'That's how mate!' He would only have laughed!

I missed the next nine matches through injury, including a 2–0 fifth round home win against Swansea and a nail-biting quarter-final KO at Upton Park of a Division One Villa managed by old Charlton team-mate Ron Saunders.

Ron and I shook hands before the game but did not see each other after it – events doubtless giving Ron other things to do! For, like the Albion tie at The Hawthorns, the match seemed to confirm it was West Ham's Wembley year again. With a minute to go and no score, we were resigned to a Villa Park replay. Then Villa's Ken McNaught inexplicably stuck his hand up to a nothing high ball in their box.

I bet to this day he cannot explain why he did it. An experienced, competent centre-back, he must have known Villa had all but secured the replay. Perhaps he had the mistaken idea that somebody had got round the back and was on for a header. But it was right under the ref's nose. Many probably missed it.

Watching from the stand, I had a clear view but, even so, could hardly believe I'd seen such a blatant hand-ball.

Villa's goalkeeper was the excellent Jimmy Rimmer, who'd been on the losing Arsenal side at Highbury five years earlier when we beat them on our way to the final. What his thoughts were as he faced up to Tonka's last-minute penalty I cannot imagine. I know what Ray's were. First minute, last minute, last second even ... Ray never lets the situation get to him. 'I'd rather be taking a penalty than not taking one' is his attitude. If I had my pick of the whole League, there's nobody I would choose before Ray for spot-kicks.

There was a period when, as captain, I shouldered that responsibility, and when the pressure was on the old butterflies really started for me. Ray seems utterly nerve-less and, in fact, the more tense the position the better he appears to enjoy it.

Many present just could not bear to watch him with that so-vital one against Villa. I would have bet our house on him scoring – and he did.

We still went to Villa Park. That was the venue for the semi-final against more Division One opposition, Everton. They were an excellent side, but it was still the best draw for us, leaving Liverpool and Arsenal to meet in the other semi.

The two games we fought out with Everton to get to Wembley remain among the best I've ever played in – or had personally. The first, at Villa, was in total contrast to that non-event against Ipswich in the 1975 semi-final on the same ground. Both sides played attacking, open football, each firmly convinced they had the beating of the other. Everton led through a Brian Kidd penalty close to half-time. The award by ref Colin Seel upset us, but not as much as a later ruling, after Stuart Pearson had equalised in the second half.

As things heated up at 1–1, Kiddie got himself sent off. Then with not long to go little Ollie beat Martin Hodge and we were certain it was Wembley again. But, to our disbelief, Mr Seel disallowed the goal for off-side – not against Ollie but Trevor, who was out wide on a flank nowhere near the action. I've already commented earlier how Ollie cried after the final. When that goal was ruled out there were tears in his eyes – tears of rage!

The replay, at Leeds the following Wednesday, produced an even better match. Brian Kidd was automatically banned, following his sending-off. His absence was good news for us – but I was later to view it somewhat differently!

The game was goal-less after ninety minutes. Early in extra-time Dev, who was absolutely brilliant all through, scored a spectacular goal after beating what seemed like half the Everton side. Seven minutes from time Bob Latchford shattered us with an equaliser. I can see him now, running to the Everton fans behind our goal, and hanging by both hands from the top of the fencing, literally snarling in triumph.

But cometh the hour.... With just a couple of minutes to go Frank Lampard, who hadn't played in the first game, turned up in Everton's area to win the match with a diving header. Usually a laid-back type, much in the Mooro mould, Frank gave a rare display of personal emotion when that went in. None of us could catch him as he sprinted hell-for-leather to a corner flag, around which he danced an ecstatic little jig. When I eventually reached him, I said: 'What the hell were you doing up in their box, Frank?' He just smiled happily and replied: 'I dunno.'

In the after-match celebrations it doesn't really sink in that you are actually at Wembley. I remember relaxing in the Elland Road players' lounge, sitting alongside Ollie. Not yet eighteen, he looked little more than a schoolboy then. That cherubic face had a kind of dazed smile on it. 'How are you feeling, Ollie?' I enquired. He stared at me as if seeing nothing and simply murmured: 'Magic, Bonzo, magic!'

It certainly was that night. The coach journey home from Leeds had never gone so quickly. But I was very soon in dire need of some real magic.

A couple of games later we faced Birmingham in the League at Upton Park in mid-week. They were fourth in the table, just a point off the pace. we were eight points behind the leaders but, with three games in hand, still well in the promotion stakes. Earlier in the month we'd shared a goal-less draw at St Andrew's. The return game was our first at home after beating Everton, and over 37,000 crammed in for it.

So the atmosphere was white-hot and, though Wembley was just round the corner, there was nothing half-hearted in our approach. Birmingham went ahead but Alvin equalised soon after the interval. Then suddenly I was on the floor with Brum's former England defender Colin Todd. We kicked out at each other, then got up to swap blows. Referee Alan Gunn had no option but to send off both of us.

It was an incident I will be always ashamed of. Experienced senior pros, Toddie and me should have known better. By the time we reached the tunnel we both realised what bloody fools we looked. But it was not until I sat in the empty dressing-room that it suddenly dawned on me that my mad moment could not only have put Hammers out of the promotion chase – but also myself out of the Cup final! I realised what a right berk I'd been.

It was Tuesday, 22 April. The final was on 10 May. So close that I surely had to be suspended on the big day. With Birmingham winning 2–1 that night, there were long faces about in the home dressing-room.

If I had set out to make things as difficult as possible I could not have succeeded more. Quite apart from the question of what it might mean for the club, not knowing if I would be able to play at Wembley caused obvious personal problems. None of the family knew whether or not to prepare for a big day out, with all the necessary attendant arrangements.

I suffered agonies of self-recrimination.

West Ham appealed against the sending-off and John Lyall and I had to go to the FA for the hearing. Imagine how I felt when it turned out that chairman of the appeal Committee was ... Bert Millichip! It was his Albion we'd beaten in the third round of the competition the previous January – the game where my tug on big Regis had so annoyed their chairman. Now my fate was in his hands. I'd already served the automatic one-game ban following the Birmingham match, but additional suspension seemed certain.

When John and I went into the appeal it seemed to me from the way he looked at me that Mr Millichip had a life ban in mind. But they decided the one-game suspension already served was enough. I was clear to play at Wembley.

I gave a heart-felt silent prayer of thanks, got through as quickly as possible the inevitable press corps questions, then rushed out of Lancaster Gate to find the nearest phone. Luckily it was working and I got through to Lyn and yelled: 'I'm OK, I'm OK!'

18

That Arsenal Cup final left egg on quite a few faces . . . including mine! For only this year did I realise that, as in 1975 when we beat Fulham, I again managed totally to ignore my club chairman, the late Reg Pratt, as I went up to the royal box to receive the trophy.

I found this out from some film clips of those two finals given to me by Henry Champ, London man for the American NBC network, along with a video of the programme they made when I got the MBE. These show Reg, standing close to the Duke and Duchess of Kent, smiling happily at his captain as I arrive at the top of the stairs – but yours truly just walks straight past him as if he wasn't there!

Reg Pratt was the very last man I would have ever done that to knowingly. He was the best of club chairmen, one who never interfered on the football side but was West Ham through and through. Fortunately, on each Cup final occasion we had plenty of opportunity at the celebrations in the evening to exchange congratulations . . . and it was typical of Reg that neither time did he mention that I'd not noticed him as I went up to get the Cup.

The night before the Arsenal final Trevor and I sat watching television in our hotel. There was a programme on previewing the game and we were really needled by some comments made by Alan Mullery, who had led Fulham against us in our previous Wembley appearance five years earlier.

Among the reasons Mullers advanced as to why he felt West Ham would not win the next day was that Alvin Martin and I did not compare as centre-backs with the Gunners' David O'Leary and Willie Young. They were in a different class, he reckoned.

Well, football will always be a matter of opinion. But it was the same the following season when Hammers ran away with the Second Division championship – and Malcolm Macdonald informed readers in a newspaper article that Billy Bonds just would not last the pace back in the First Division. That was eight years ago now!

That kind of thing never really bothers me. All it does is to gee me up to be even more determined to prove points in the only place they count . . . out there on the park.

But you wouldn't be human not to notice at all when people who do not know you come out with views like that. To me, it seems all they do is base their ideas on their own standards of fitness. 'Billy Bonds – 32 isn't he?' And because may be the end of their particular road was in sight when they were around that age, you are placed in the same category.

If they took the trouble to talk to you, find out how you felt physically and mentally, came and watched you train, asked around among team-mates and opponents – then they might avoid the risk of looking ill-informed.

Stretch and I needed no motivation for the Arsenal final. But that 'different class' remark by Mullers put the finishing edge to our attitude.

We woke up the next morning to find some equally damning remarks from Brian Clough in a newspaper. The Forest manager, paraphrasing Muhammad Ali, declared that Trevor 'stung like a butterfly'. Typically, Trevor did not say a lot about it, but I could tell he was really steamed up. Like Stretch and me, he required no further motivating after that.

Maybe, Cloughie did it for that reason. Perhaps he was on the side of the underdogs and felt a little wind-up like that would get us going even more than we were already. If that had nothing to do with what was printed under his name, though, I only hope he'd put his money where his mouth was . . . for Trev went out, played a blinder, and stung all right with that headed winner!

The game itself was a chess-board affair of almost purely tactical football, low on incident and excitement, very different from those flowing semi-final thrillers with Everton.

Arsenal had qualified for the final only after three gruelling tussles against Liverpool. They were also going well in the League and the UEFA Cup.

Their line-up included Liam Brady, who had played in that

So important, a secure, loving home life. Dad holds younger brother Mick in one arm and tries to stop me being camera-shy with the other. We are at the London Transport sports ground, where Dad would have been playing . . . but for the broken right leg he has in plaster.

The first-ever Billy Bonds goal – I wonder? Close on three years of age, I make a blind-side run past Mum, who has her arms full dealing with off-side claims from eighteen-months old Mick. But, with the net at my mercy, I seem more interested in the contents of that bag in my right hand . . . so perhaps I didn't score, after all.

The Middle Park Junior School team of 1956–57, as the ball I'm holding announces. Mr Collins (left) and Mr Evans are the teachers, both putting in much time and effort with us.

The Woolwich district Under-15 team. As usual, I've got the ball.

(*Above left*) Happy holiday snap – with Mick and me making sure Dad isn't going to have a quiet look at his paper.
(*Above right*) First time in the claret-and-blue for me. Two days after signing for West Ham I made my 'début' in Ken Brown's testimonial match at Upton Park. This shot was taken during the pre-game kick-in.

The Charlton Athletic youth squad. Of those in the picture, Alan Campbell (far left, front), Ray Keeley (on my left), Dennis Booth (next to Ray), Vic Halom (second from the right, back) and Stewart Scullion (far right, front) all had careers in the game. Coach Jock Basford, the man who helped me so much, is far right in the back row, behind manager Frank Hill.

New boy Bonds already looks very much at home as he jokes with Eddie Bov' (left) and thumbs-up Harry Redknapp on the coach leaving Upton Park for a first-ever trip abroad with Hammers, back in 1967.

Leeds' England defender Terry Cooper seems almost as concerned as Martin Peters and yours truly as we argue with referee Mr T. A. Pallister about the sending-off of Harry Redknapp at Elland Road in October 1968.

Lyn was an even more radiant than usual bride on our 1967 wedding day . . . as Harry Redknapp, the bridegroom, Jimmy Lindsay and Trevor Brooking sport deep tans gained on a West Ham summer tour to America. As here, best man H kept his hands in his pockets all day!

Chelsea always seemed to be a lucky club for me. Here's one of my goals against them at The Bridge watched by Peter Houseman, Eddie McCreadie and Chopper Harris. This was on 9 September 1972, on a day Hammers won 3–1 . . . with all our goals coming from the half-back line as Mooro and Tommy Taylor joined me on the scoring list. But now I can't believe I ever got up this high!

(*Left*) The one and only hat-trick of my career came against Chelsea, on 2 March 1974, at Upton Park. This was one of the trio, a header as I climb above Chopper Harris.

(*Below*) And that makes three! Trevor Brooking watches as I volley my third goal past Peter Bonetti to complete a hat-trick.

(*Right*) Celebrations with the South Bank fans after that hat-trick goal. Peter Bonetti sits out the racket – and you can just see his team-mate Johnny Hollins in the background.

(*Below*) When I nod my head . . .! Anything goes when you've just won the cup – and I'm only too ready to oblige joker Tommy Taylor!

Mooro and me with the FA Cup at Upton Park on the Monday after the 1975 win over Fulham . . . the occasion was the testimonal match for West Ham's much respected chief scout Wally St Pier.

Don't ask me what we are celebrating . . . but it must have been a bit special for Frankie Lampard and me to hug each other like this!

fifth round Highbury tie five years before. Chippy has since become a West Ham team-mate, via several top Italian clubs, and he admits these days that the Gunners, with so many games already behind them that season, went to Wembley physically and mentally tired. Certainly, class strikers like Frank Stapleton and Alan Sunderland gave us few of the problems we expected.

Arsenal just never seemed to figure out exactly how to counter John Lyall's surprise tactics of playing only David Cross as an orthodox striker and having Stuart Pearson in a withdrawn role in the hole behind him. The risk for us in such a gambit is that the opposition, with never more than a two-on-four threat to their own defence, might push players forward from the back. Crossie did a lot of unselfish running, hardly seeing the ball as he chased about that sapping Wembley turf. But even when our tactics were clear, Arsenal unaccountably still did not try to get people forward from the back. I think it was not until the last fifteen minutes or so that David O'Leary began to come forward a bit. By then we had long been in front from the kind of goal that so often wins finals.

Dev was at the start of the move which brought it, but there were two West Ham shots going nowhere before Trevor stooped to get his head to the second and deflect it past Pat Jennings. The ball was veering well wide across goal until Trev's head intervened, and I'm sure he could not believe it when the ball went in.

With Arsenal so punch-less on the day, it proved the winner. We might have had another when 'Ollie' – Paul Allen, the youngest-ever player to appear in an FA Cup final – broke through but was tripped right on the edge of the area by Willie Young. It was around the time of so much being made of the 'professional' foul. The big Scot was booked for his offence, and some felt he was lucky not to go off.

Least upset by that particular incident was the victim, Ollie. It seemed big Willie's professional foul had robbed Ollie of a Wembley Cup final goal, but our teenager pointed out afterwards: 'I still had to beat Pat Jennings, and that's not easy, is it?' There's honesty for you!

After the presentation of the Cup, the lap of honour, the high jinks and laughter in the dressing-room, I spent those few moments alone back up the tunnel taking in and savouring the scene. Then it was off to our London hotel in the team coach to get ready for the evening's celebration banquet. But in the end I found myself short on time getting spruced up for the dinner after being called on to give a helping hand elsewhere.

Rob Jenkins just never got to the dinner at all. It was a repeat of the 1975 final night affair for both of us, as I tucked him up in bed by 7 p.m. and left him to sleep it off.

And this time I got a second similar job. Ernie Gregory, our long-serving goalkeeper coach, had supped deeply out of the Cup on the way from Wembley to the hotel – too deeply for someone who rarely touches alcohol. Lyn and I were in a room next to Ernie and his wife and could hear him singing cheerfully away at 'We are the West Ham Boys' and 'Bubbles'. Mrs Gregory was soon knocking on our door for help, worried sick that Ernie would not make it to the dinner. The pair of us finally managed to get him on to the bed and, with plenty of black coffee, dressed in his best whistle. But it was a very quiet, white-faced Ernie who sat through the evening!

After a marvellous evening, Lyn and I, still too wound-up to sleep, decided to take a short, small-hours stroll with a friend and his wife up to the Ritz Hotel's casino and see if West Ham's luck was still in. It wasn't, because the man on the door would not let us in. He must have been an Arsenal fan! Just as well, really – he probably saved me a few bob!

The Sunday morning brought an unforgettable coach ride through East London with the Cup. There seemed to be even more people thronging the streets than I remembered in 1975. Even with a police escort it took ages and, once again, we realised just what winning the Cup means to people.

By the time Lyn and I finally got home that Sunday we were very tired. But we were hardly indoors when the phone went. It was my old mate Pop Robson, calling from the north-east with his congratulations.

There was, however, a little more to it. Pop was then having his second spell with Sunderland – and we were due to play our final League game of the season at Roker the following night. Sunderland needed to win to pip Chelsea for promotion. So Pop was anxious to remind me of this, and to enquire just how worn-out we might be after Wembley! I said we were certainly very tired, but there was no chance of us giving them an easy ride to Division One.

The Roker crowd, there in strength for what they hoped would be a big occasion for them, applauded us when we ran out at the start – a nice gesture. They were not quite so complimentary when we came close to going ahead; nor when it was still 0–0 at half-time, despite intense Sunderland pressure.

As we walked off at the interval Pop's face revealed his worries. To me, the little fella was among the best strikers I've played with and against, desperately unlucky to miss out on England honours. He also had no luck at all, in some respects, with his moves between his native north-east and West Ham. Three times he transferred one way or the other the season before an FA Cup final win. As we went in at half-time that night he clearly suspected he was going to miss out again. For a draw was not going to be enough to put Sunderland up.

'Don't look so worried, Pop, the way it's going you are bound to get one,' I told him. In the end they got two, and were promoted. But nobody could say the Cup winners did not make them play all the way for it.

After the game I went into the home dressing-room to congratulate Pop and Frank Clark and the rest of the Sunderland lads, and wish them well in Division One the next season. 'We'll be joining you soon,' I said. And we did a season later.

19

As Cup holders we figured in the traditional FA Charity Shield 'curtain-raiser' the following season, meeting First Division champs Liverpool at Wembley. We were to face the same opponents there seven months later in the League Cup final. I was by then well into what I now look back on as my 'second' career, the one in which it all really happened, after those seasons which earned no honours at club level.

Honestly, I often find it almost impossible to get it all in perspective and sequence. Only since I started on this autobiography have I myself begun to appreciate just how long I've actually been around.

It's been brought forcibly home at times when I've found myself player against the sons of former team-mates from way back! After a reserve game against QPR last season, for instance, one of their youngsters came up to me and said: 'Dad asked me to pass on his regards, Billy.' Playing at second-team level you rarely bother about taking a pre-match look at the opposition's team-sheet, so I had to admit I wasn't sure who the young Ranger was referring to. But when he explained he was Gavin Peacock I at once realised the dad involved must be the Keith Peacock who was an established Charlton player when I first got into the side there.

Another time, at Spurs, Richard Gough went out of his way to seek me out before the game and similarly pass on his father's best wishes. I already knew the Tottenham signing from Scotland was the son of another old Valley club-mate, Charlie Gough, whom we always knew as 'Chopper', though not for the same reasons as Ron Harris! I appreciated his son's contact ... especially as it came before rather than after the game. We got stuffed 5–0! To youngsters like that I must seem like Rip Van Winkle.

The 1975 Cup final, I suppose, marked the start of my 'second' career. After it, I returned to Wembley on another four occasions, played in a European competition final, and won a Second Division championship medal – all when I was past 28. Yet almost a decade before the League Cup final against Liverpool I honestly began to think I would never play at Wembley at all.

In the early seventies I reckon I was at my peak. I felt strong, full of running, able to motor flat out all through any game. Yet I got not a single tangible reward from those best years.

The closest we came to anything was in 1971–72, when we lost to Stoke in the League Cup semi-finals after no fewer than four tussles – games which I can still vividly recall and which were certainly among the best I played in. We were absolutely shattered when we finally lost in a second replay. Though only in my mid-twenties, I thought at that time it was the nearest I would ever get to Wembley. I somehow had the uneasy suspicion there was not much longer left for me to win anything!

The Stoke defeat was a real sickener, because the prize seemed to be snatched away after it had been virtually in our grasp. We already felt it was 'our' year after winning two early round ties, despite being taken to replays on opposition grounds.

Cardiff held us 1–1 at Upton Park in the second round, and were obviously hopeful of completing the giant-killing at Ninian Park. Over 30,000 turned up to cheer a Welsh win ... but we beat them 2–1.

Leeds visited us in the fourth round, just four days after we had played a goal-less draw in the League at Elland Road. A similar result in the League Cup took us back to Leeds, with the odds very much on them, but a goal from the big man, Clyde Best, put us through.

In the next round we got a home draw – against Liverpool who, in those days, fielded the likes of Ray Clemence, Tommy Smith, Emlyn Hughes, Kevin Keegan, Steve Heighway, John Toshack and Ian Callaghan. You realise how things have changed now when the records show that nearly 41,000 crammed in for that game, which ended with a 2–1 West Ham win.

We were at home in the quarter-finals to Sheffield United, who a little earlier had won 2–1 at Upton Park in the League. The Blades came back, now fourth in Division One, but were blasted by a Pop Robson hat-trick and two from Clyde.

This put us in the semis, with a first leg visit to Stoke, who had lost 2–1 on our ground in the League three months earlier. Playing away first suited us fine, because then you know what has to be done in the return, when home advantage is on your side. We trailed early on at Stoke, but when a Geoff Hurst penalty and a second-half goal from Clyde gave us a 2–1 win, it looked as if we had the job more than half done.

Geoff fired that spot-kick past his old England World Cup winning team-mate Gordon Banks with all the ferocity typical of the way he took pens – so hard that a goalkeeper risked going in with the ball if he got in the way! I never discovered if Banksie was in the habit of facing Geoff's penalties in England training. But, from the way things turned out, he certainly seemed to learn something from that one up at Stoke.

A fortnight later Stoke came to us for the second leg. We needed no more than a draw to be at Wembley. Not that West Ham would ever play it that way! We chased forward all over the place from the start and looked like scoring several. But Banks and some wayward finishing kept us out, and lofty John Ritchie poached a goal for Stoke to go ahead seventeen minutes from the end and make it 2–2 on aggregate.

In almost the last minute Stoke went mad when the ref ruled that their brilliant goalkeeper had brought down my mate 'Arry boy in the area.

For the second time in the two games Gordon Banks faced a Geoff Hurst penalty ... and now everything hinged on it. If Geoff scored, West Ham were Wembley bound.

I don't mind admitting I was among the many of the close on 39,000 present who just could not bear to watch! As Geoff ran up to take the kick I half turned away, unable to look. So I never actually watched what hundreds have since told me was the finest penalty save they have ever witnessed. I saw only a turned-over ball flying up into the fans on the north bank – and then Banksie being submerged under a mass of jubilant, relieved team-mates.

The old England star is always remembered most for the save he made from Pele in the 1970 World Cup ... but by West Ham for the penalty stop which denied us a trip to Wembley. There were plenty wise after the event, who reckoned we should have had someone else taking the kick, in case Banksie guessed right after being beaten by Geoff's effort at Stoke. But, like Tonka today, Geoff rarely missed. The pace of his shot was usually more than enough, and that night it had to go down as a marvellous save, not a missed penalty, underlining what we all knew ... that Gordon Banks was the best goalkeeper in the world!

His save took the tie into extra time, but this brought no further score and it ended 1–0 to Stoke, making it 2–2 on aggregate and a third game necessary.

After some argument about venue and kick-off time, this was fixed for Hillsborough, nearly three times as far from Upton Park as from Stoke. But Mooro and Hurstie, at least, did not mind going back to the ground where they had helped Hammers beat Manchester United in the FA Cup semi-final seven years earlier.

The tie drew another huge gate, almost 47,000. Congestion around the ground was such that both teams had problems getting there.

We stayed at a hotel in Buxton and our coach journey into Sheffield was frightening. Traffic was bumper-to-bumper solid, and the coach took at least four knocks forcing a way through. When we did arrive, however, we were fifteen minutes ahead of Stoke, whose vehicle was involved in a collision en route! All round, it was not a good night for the West Ham team coach. It would not start after the match ... and it was later discovered that somebody had tipped a bag of sugar into the petrol tank!

The match was another razor-close struggle but finished without a goal, extending the tie into a real saga.

But despite three such nerve-tingling encounters, the real drama was still to come. Old Trafford was named for the second replay – a choice which again seemed to favour our Midlands opponents. Six train-loads of Hammers followers, however, were among the 49,000 who saw a match which put the previous three in the shade.

Manchester treated us to the kind of weather for which it is infamous: belting rain all through and a nasty, swirling wind.

With only fifteen minutes gone disaster hit us when goalkeeper Bobby Ferguson went down at Terry Conroy's feet – and didn't get up. Fester had taken a fearful, accidental kick on the head. He lay on the pitch for over five minutes having treatment from Rob Jenkins before staggering back into goal. But play had hardly restarted when Mooro was demanding that referee Pat Partridge stop it again. Fester was reeling about like a drunk, obviously in no fit state to continue.

He was led off, leaving us with the awkward dilemma of whether to play on ten-strong in the hope that he would come back, or to put the sub on and play the rest of the match with an outfield player as makeshift goalkeeper. For such an important game it had to be the first option, and we all looked round for Clyde Best to take over in goal until Fester returned – if he did. The big striker was always the pre-match choice for this role and, in fact, had done it previously when Fester was hurt on another occasion.

But this time the big man bottled it. I can see him now, with panic in his eyes, clearly not fancying the job. Mooro took a real skipper's decision. 'Give us the jumper,' he declared – and went in goal himself.

Almost immediately he must have wished he had not. For Stoke were awarded a penalty when John McDowell, trying to retrieve the position when his back-pass held up in the mud, up-ended John Ritchie.

I remember Frankie Lampard standing near me, as Mick Bernard put the ball on the spot, and muttering: 'Mooro's got so much schmozzle he'll save it!' It wasn't a bad forecast. Bobby got both hands to Bernard's kick and turned the ball out, only for the Stoke man to follow up and score off the rebound.

It was lousy luck for Mooro and us. But I think it only made our ten men go all the harder. A few minutes later I equalised and then went away on a right-wing run and crossed for Trevor to put us in front with a superb left-foot volley.

When Fester came back after being off for twenty minutes, it seemed fortune was running our way. But what we didn't know was that, after being brought round in the dressing-room, Fester had been taken out into the tunnel where Ron Greenwood and Rob chucked balls at him, trying to decide if he was fit to go back on. We later learned that, while Fester's handling seemed normal, he could not answer when they asked if he knew where he was and what the match was. Still badly concussed, he hadn't a clue!

It was typically brave of him to insist on going back on. One quality Fester was never short on was courage. But it was quickly plain that he was very wobbly. In the minutes just before and just after the break, Stoke scored twice to go back in front – Fester's reactions each time well late. I doubt if either shot would have got past him had he been in full possession of his faculties.

After that, we did everything but save the game. A well-beaten Banks was rescued by an upright, and Pat Partridge must have been the only one in the ground who did not think an Alan Bloor challenge on Geoff worth a penalty. Beaten 3–2, we were utterly drained, physically and emotionally, after the whistle.

I could not believe it. Sitting in the dressing-room, chin on chest, I thought: 'Just what do you have to do to get to Wembley?' I was sure my last chance had gone out of the window.

The press was full of praise for our display and how we fought against misfortune. But it still had not been enough.

All my folks were at the game, Mum and Dad, Lyn and her parents, and when I got back home they were all positive we deserved to have gone through over the four games, which remain among the best I recall.

It was Stoke, however, and not us who were there for the big day. And I was sure they would win, too! A goal down after the first leg at home; a fantastic penalty save right at the death to give them an unlikely reprieve; a goal-less first replay draw; and then all the fortune in the second replay at Old Trafford. Yet again a great example of the old business of your name being on the Cup!

Few thought the same as me before the final. Stoke's opponents were Chelsea, who beat Spurs in the other semi and had such fine players as Peter Osgood, Johnny Hollins, Ron Harris, Peter Houseman, Dave Webb and Alan Hudson. They were the hottest of favourites for the trophy. But Stoke won 2–1.

We still had to go to Stoke for a League game after their first-ever trophy triumph. We took a goal-less draw to make that semi-final choker even harder to swallow. West Ham finished in mid-table and went out of the FA Cup at Huddersfield in the fifth round, after surviving an earlier scare at little Hereford. About the only satisfaction from the season was a double over Spurs.

I played every game that season sixteen years ago. As I said before, it was the period when I felt in my prime, able to run all day no problem, challenge hard, and also play a bit. But I still had nothing to show for it.

When I think about how I played then, I have a quiet smile these days when I hear team-mates, who were only babies at that time, being complimentary about me. If they think Bonzo gets stuck in now, they should have seen him then!

20

Any worries I had back in those days that time was running out for me fortunately proved totally misplaced. By the time we faced Liverpool in the 1980–81 League Cup final, Hammers were romping away with the Second Division title, breaking all kinds of records, and, despite an early exit as FA Cup holders, were also going well in Europe.

It was my fifth club outing at Wembley – some turnabout for a guy who believed his last chance gone nine years earlier – and the match proved the most controversial of the lot.

After beating Third Division Burnley 6–0 on aggregate over two legs in the first round, we went back to my old club Charlton in the next, where we won a tight game 2–1 with a late goal from Crossie.

Barnsley proved even harder to overcome in the next round at Upton Park, going ahead through their tall centre-half Ian Evans before our own number five Stretch scored the equaliser, quickly followed by another winner from Crossie.

'Psycho' did it again in the following round, netting near the end to put out First Division Spurs at Upton Park – when our London rivals were making all the headlines after signing Ardiles and Villa from Argentine.

We were away to more Division One opposition, Coventry, in the first leg of the semi-final. Seldom have I come away from any game with such mixed feelings. Before it, I suppose we would have settled readily enough to have only a one-goal deficit to make up in the return home leg, especially as West Ham were then on a run of thirteen successive League and cup wins at Upton Park. In fact, an opening day defeat against Luton turned out to be the only League game we lost at home that winter. But we left Highfield Road very much aware we had made that second leg task needlessly more tricky – by letting a two-goal interval lead slip away.

Our first goal must rank as the most wonky I ever scored. I

was forward to get my head to a ball inside the box, but there was little power behind the header and it presented Coventry goalkeeper Les Sealey with no apparent problems ... until he let the ball slip through his hands and over the line.

If that was lucky for us, the second was even more unlikely. Gary Thompson, the Sky Blues' big, powerful striker, rushed back to help out in defence and, with Dev challenging, sent a back-pass past Sealey.

In those situations the idea is always to frustrate the anticipated opposition rally for the first fifteen minutes or so after the restart. Coventry threw everything at us, but it looked like coming to nothing when the game passed the hour with the score unchanged. But within six minutes they were level through Thompson and Gerry Daly. Even then, we seemed certain to come away with a highly respectable draw ... until Thompson made up for that earlier unlikely own-goal with an injury-time winner, to complete a tremendous comeback by his team. This dramatic turn-around was a bitter disappointment for us.

When Coventry visited us the big danger was of going even further behind on aggregate and having too much to do. We might have done so very early on, but the lanky Mark Hateley volleyed over from one of the best chances Coventry had all night.

Paul Goddard finally broke the deadlock on the hour to make it 3–3. But with away goals not counting in this competition, we still faced extra time and a possible replay – with all the overtones of that Stoke affair which no one at West Ham had forgotten.

Sarge and Crossie had already plundered 39 goals between them that season. Jimmy Neighbour had just one – albeit the only goal to beat Cardiff at home. But it was Jimbo who turned up round the back of Coventry's defence to slip in a last-minute winner and put us at Wembley for the second season running.

Little Jimbo was always among the most popular men among team-mates ... but never more so than that night! Coventry were to wait a bit longer for their own first trophy win.

The final was Arsenal all over again for us. As before, we were the Division Two underdogs against a top First Division club.

Liverpool were English and European champions. The League Cup was the only trophy they had never won. And for Clemence and Steve Heighway the final was even more significant: they were the sole survivors from the Liverpool team we put out of the competition nine years earlier on our way to those semi-final ding-dongs with Stoke!

But Hammers' right to the First Division place they resumed the following season was more than proved as we battled hard to go through ninety tense goal-less minutes with them.

All that really mattered finally came in the last few seconds of extra time, which produced the controversy for which the game is now most remembered. Liverpool had already had a goal disallowed earlier in the game because a player was in an off-side position. Three minutes from the finish Alan Kennedy hammered the ball past Phil Parkes – but little Sammy Lee, lying yards off-side, had to duck his head to let it rocket over him en route. Referee Clive Thomas, however, allowed the goal, despite our furious protests ... and his own previous opposite ruling in very much the same situation. It looked like a winner which would set up a rare old rumpus afterwards.

In the final minute we won a free-kick and did the obvious last desperate ploy by sending Stretch up into their box, in the hope that he would use his strength in the air. He responded with a thundering close-range header which left Clemence helpless – and the on-the-line Terry McDermott with no option but to fist the ball over the bar.

It was another last-seconds penalty ordeal for Tonka, this time with 100,000 looking at him. I made sure I watched, too. Cool as ever, Ray fired the spot-kick past Clemence for an equaliser that was rich justice after the bitter dispute over Liverpool's goal.

The final whistle went almost immediately, and, for someone who was normally in the thick of things, I somehow seemed to miss out on the barney that erupted after the game. I think I was probably looking round for some guidance as to whether or not the teams would still go up to the box, even though a replay meant there would be no trophy presentation. Anyway, I was hardly even aware of the exchange of words between John Lyall and Clive Thomas, and did not realise until we were in the dressing-room that our manager had been booked. It all related, of course, to the unsatisfactory nature of the Liverpool goal which, despite the last-gasp second chance we'd gained, still left us fuming.

When Kennedy's shot went in I know I gestured angrily at the linesman, urging him to get his flag up. But it was one occasion when I perhaps did not persist too long with protests . . . because long experience had taught me that one thing Clive Thomas never did was change a decision.

The Welshman was always regarded by many as a controversial figure. Yet I considered him a good ref, largely because you knew where you were with him. Once he made a ruling, then that was that: no amount of arguing would alter his mind. And, for players, consistency by refs is at least a definite attitude.

In this case Clive Thomas definitely got it wrong. If he had disallowed that earlier Liverpool goal for off-side, then he had to do the same for Kennedy's effort.

The upshot was that neither side took the glory on the day. Both teams visited the royal box to shake hands with the guest of honour, Football League president Lord Westwood.

Nowadays, a replay would almost certainly be staged at Wembley again. But that one went on at Villa Park, delayed almost three weeks because of both clubs' European commitments. Villa's HQ is a splendid ground, but it's not quite the same as playing at Wembley.

We shook Liverpool by going ahead early on with a Sarge header, but they finally won 2–1 to take the League Cup for the first time.

For me and some of our side it was the second time we'd lost in a final – the first being the European Cup Winners' Cup in Brussels. All you can do is to try and show dignity in defeat, but you certainly have little trouble making yourself as small as possible while the winners are rushing about celebrating! And it did not seem quite as bad as losing at Wembley. Nor was it anything like as sickening, to me at least, as that Stoke semi-final defeat some years ealier. After all, we had actually got to the final.

Doing so had made a lot of money for the club, especially with a final replay. Happily, too, John's booking did not get him into trouble. In fact, the man who came out of it not too well was Clive Thomas, since there were any number of witnesses – and film evidence – to confirm that he approached John first, so any words which passed between them were the result of our manager answering the referee rather than diving in himself. John was completely exonerated by the FA.

21

It is commonplace for players to praise their own fans as the best in the country, but I am quite sure that ours played a big part in helping us reach the 1975–76 European Cup Winners' Cup final.

We had fortune with us in that campaign, since in every round the first leg tie was away from home. In fact, we never won on foreign soil. But we did enough to always have a shout in the return game at Upton Park. And our supporters on those memorable nights were worth a goal start to us, in my view! The atmosphere they generated was tremendous, better even than for the FA Cup. Playing in our tight, compact ground, a cauldron of noise, with leather-lunged East-enders breathing down their necks, was a totally new experience for most of the visitors. Some clearly bottled it.

West Ham were no strangers to the competition, having won it in a classic 1965 Wembley final against TSV Munich 1860 and gone to the semi-finals the following season. I watched that Munich sparkler on television, never suspecting I would be a Hammer myself two years later and go on to lead them back into Europe.

It fulfilled another long-time ambition of mine, playing in Europe. It gave me the opportunity not only of facing at club level the different Continental approach, but also of getting to several far-flung places I would never have seen otherwise.

At times English teams have tended to make a fuss about how tiring European competition can be, with often long hauls fitted in between domestic League games. The travelling can certainly prove gruelling, particularly to places like Russia. But such trips are also a welcome change from ordinary routine. You go out on the Monday, train the next day in new surroundings, play the tie on the Wednesday, fly back home the next day, and then have a brief training session on the Friday before your next

League game. It is all a marked contrast to the chores of normal weekly practice.

West Ham were fortunate to be eased back into Europe in 1975 with a kind opening game, the draw taking us to the part-timers of Finnish club Lahden Reipas – hardly difficult opposition for an English First Division side.

We flew out to Helsinki confident they would present us with few problems. But we soon found out the days were past when Scandinavian teams, even the minnows, could be dismissed as 6–0 pushovers! Soccer is not the big attraction in Finland, where the real interest is in winter sports and athletics. Our game was played in the spacious Olympic stadium, but with only 6,000 spectators present. Which for us was just as well.

We did ourselves scant justice and were trailing 2–1 until I played a one-two with Patsy Holland to grab a late, face-saving equaliser. I had the satisfaction of scoring in my first European competition match, but it was about the only joy I got from an occasion which suggested West Ham might not be going far. But it at least taught us the immense value in Europe of coming back home with something tangible goal-wise. The Finns lost 3–0 at Upton Park a fortnight later as we played much more to expected form.

The next round draw had us scratching heads and asking: 'Who? – where?' Again we played away first, this time to Russia's Ararat Erevan in Armenia. None of us had ever heard of them or had much clue where it actually was. But all our friends in English football were quick to warn us that they would prove tough opposition.

The hotel we stayed in out there was overlooked by Mount Ararat, where, according to the Bible, the Ark came to rest. Frankly, that was about all the place had going for it. A real dive it turned out. There were more cockroaches in the rooms than guests, and the decor wasn't helped by peeling wallpaper everywhere.

As usual, I roomed with Trevor and in one drawer of the dressing-table we discovered some bread and cheese that looked – and smelt – as if it had been there since the Ark was up on that looming mountain. The bread was hard and heavy enough to be used in a field event – probably shot-putting –

while the cheese would have curled the whiskers of even those whopping rats I'd known in my days at The Valley! In the circumstances it was hardly surprising I had a very disturbed night. Trev pretty near always got ill on such trips. This was no exception. He spent most of the night alternating between filling the sink and dashing to the loo. It proved a good way for Trevor to lose half-a-stone ... but he was never going to play in the match. He was so bad, in fact, that he could not even leave the hotel to watch.

Another alarming (to us) feature of that establishment was a huge, forbidding matron-type lady who sat, unsmiling, at a desk in the corridor on our floor. Whenever we left the room, even to go elsewhere in the hotel, we had to give her the key. She would return it when we went back. Each time this exchange took place she glared in a way that scared the life out of us. We decided the cause was that piece of bread and cheese. It really was a field-event shot ... hers! And we speculated: 'If that's one of their women, what will the men be like?'

The tie was played in a vast stadium, watched by over 66,000. Erevan quickly showed us they were a fair team, technically very good. After a hard-fought, goal-less first half, in which they hit a post, we went ahead through Sparrer. Not long after the West German ref allowed a dodgy equaliser when Mervyn Day, preparing to clear, had the ball headed out of his hands. It would definitely not have counted in England – and these days the offender almost certainly would go in the book.

Afterwards the ref, Hans Weyland, said the game had been so sporting he'd had an easy time. Obviously, he never noticed the little exchange I had with one of their blokes after a run-in where he'd tried it on. With an accompaniment of suitable gestures, I told him, 'All right, mate, don't forget you've still got to come to London. I'll be keeping an eye out for you!' He may not have understood English, but I think he got my message.

The result was again excellent for us, particularly with that so important away goal, and we left confident Erevan would be seen off at Upton Park.

The only disappointment for me came when I went out shopping to buy the usual presents I always liked to take home from abroad for Lyn and our daughter Claire (our second girl,

Katie, had not arrived at that time).

With a pocketful of roubles that were worth nothing if they went back with me, I set out for the local High Street shops. What a let-down! The only one I could find looked like a poor man's Oxfam shop. It had just two or three toys on a shelf, all coated with a year's dust. There simply wasn't anything to buy, and for once I had to go home without anything for the girls.

The people, too, were depressing. They all went around with a down-trodden manner, like peasants.

Though I use my vote at elections, I am not a political type of bloke. But even I couldn't help asking myself what kind of set-up it must be that spends loads of money on weapons when the people, at least some of them, lived like that?

The return leg at Upton Park was played on fireworks night, just to remind me that Britain has also had its 'revolutionaries'! The Armenians (we found out they were not too keen on being called Russians) clearly did not fancy it, once they stepped out in front of 30,000 Cockneys who, after their own ample arena, must have seemed within touching distance. They had their own support from London's Armenian community who, with their ethnic costumes and 'native' musical instruments, seemed more intent upon turning the occasion into one for political protest. But the visitors were obviously intimidated by the atmosphere our fans created. Compared to how they played on their own territory, they looked an indifferent side.

By half-time we were two up through Graham Paddon and Keith Robson. But a reply soon after the interval had nerves jangling, for it meant Erevan would go through on away goals if they got another. Sparrer repeated his first leg effort, however, to snuff out any fears.

This put us in the last eight. Yet again we were favoured by having to play away first. This was of real significance all through, because when we played the second leg at home we knew just exactly what was required – and with those marvellous fans behind us.

The opposition were Den Haag, who, despite winning the Dutch Cup the previous season, were not among Holland's top teams. Yet the first leg was an utter calamity for us. In a nightmare first half we went four down. Our European hopes had to be over.

We were without Boog who, once again, had picked up a stomach bug. This gave me another far from restful night – a real pest he could be as a room-mate – but that did not excuse my part in a very poor first-half display by the Hammers.

To make it worse, Den Haag were not even a good side. Technically they were far inferior to Erevan. And yet there we were, four down and, as far as we could see, the game gone beyond recall.

It was now March 1976, and our League form had slumped dramatically after a season starting with a run of nine games without defeat. But if we were not playing well, that half-time score had a lot to do with a certain Herr Rudi Gloeckner, an East German ref who, to us, had some very strange ideas. Besides giving Den Haag two penalties in that opening 45 minutes, he constantly took us out of our stride with his peculiar rulings.

At one point, he stopped play and called me to him. I'd not been near anyone so I knew it could not be for a foul. To my disbelief he got his book out and took my number. It was some moments before I realised he'd done so because I was playing, as I often did, with my socks rolled down round my ankles. Apparently, under his laws, I was improperly dressed! I had to run to the bench and get a couple of tie-ups.

I can't say it occurred to me at the time, but I reckon Herr Rudi would have had a fit if Tommy had been up to the funny hat and false nose lark he was to pull against me a few seasons later when he skippered Orient against us in the FA Cup!

Our dressing-room was not exactly the most lively place during the interval, as we all tried to take in a 4–0 deficit. But John Lyall would not let heads droop. 'All right, we're losing four–nil. But it's not over. Go back out there and get at them. We'll beat them at Upton Park no trouble, so if you can pull a goal or two back we will still be in with a shout. Go out there and attack.'

With Herr Gloeckner 'relenting' after the restart, we did exactly that. Billy Jennings scored twice – the most important goals he ever got for West Ham – and we departed defeated, but just about still in the competition.

When the Dutch came to our place the game was reffed by Karoly Palotai, who won a gold medal with Hungary at the 1967 Tokyo Olympics.

Den Haag caught the backlash of what had gone on in that first leg. We simply steamrollered them from the start, even though, having a similar compact ground of their own, they were not intimidated by playing at Upton Park in front of 30,000 partisan fans.

The game saw almost a complete reversal of the fortunes of the first leg. By half-time we led 3–0, which put us 5–4 ahead on aggregate. Sparrer and Frankie Lampard got our first two, and the third was a penalty. In those days, spot-kicks were my regular job (no Tonka then!) and I managed to put it safely away.

It turned out to be just about the most vital goal I ever scored. The Dutch pulled one back after the interval to get level at 5–5 on aggregate.

Another Dutch goal and we were out. Graham Paddon had already gone off injured, replaced by Alan Curbishley. Then we lost Tommy, Mick McGiven coming on. 'Bruising' and 'torrid' were among the descriptions later given to the remaining minutes. But the Hungarian ref did a good job overall, doubtless having played in similar no-quarter games himself, and it ended 3–1 to us. So although it was still 5–5 on aggregate, we went through to the semi-final on those two away goals Billy Jennings scored.

John Lyall deserved a lot of credit, too. It can't be any manager's dream, having to motivate a squad who are losing four nothing at half-time. He could have been forgiven if he'd simply rucked everyone rotten. Well, John obviously did some rucking during that interval at Den Haag – but he also geed-up a very disconsolate side. Reminding us that we could play, John got heads up and turned a beaten team into one which resumed determined to salvage something from the wreck. That's a real manager!

Between us and the final stood Eintracht Frankfurt, who had won the West German Cup two seasons on the trot . . . and had beaten Atletico Madrid in both legs in the second round of the Cup Winners' Cup on their way to the semi-final. A very talented team, they were known as the 'technicians from Main' – a reference to the fact that their skills did not always prosper when the ground conditions were heavy.

Their skipper was the famed Jurgen Grabowski, though his long international career was by then over. Other internationals included Willi Neuberger, Bernd Nickel and Bernd Holzenbein, a member of West Germany's 1974 World Cup winning team. And in goal was Dr Peter Kunter, an amateur international and Eintracht's regular first choice until he retired to devote more time to his profession as a dentist. He'd come back at 35 because his successor was injured.

Once more we played the first leg away. Almost 40,000 were in the Wald Stadium – and had a nasty shock after only nine minutes when Graham Paddon fired a superb 25-yarder past the Doctor with that lethal left foot of his. Neuberger equalised midway through the first half, and a goal right after the interval by international Wolfgang Kraus made the final score 2–1 to the Germans. It was a splendid result for us – only one down and, again, a vital away goal in the bag.

I also remember the game well because it was the first time I played sweeper. I was in my thirtieth year and, I suppose, Ron Greenwood and John Lyall had it in mind that I would eventually move into the back four out of midfield. I had no worries about the switch but was very sorry for Kevin Lock, who was left out in the reshuffle. I told him this, but Kev took it tremendously and wished me all the best – showing not for the first time what a fine club man he was.

Upton Park bulged at the seams for the return leg, which remains to this day among my fondest memories.

One thing we knew for certain before the game: a German side would not suffer from the intimidating atmosphere. But, as against Den Haag, we simply 'bombed' Eintracht from the start. They managed only one corner against what seemed umpteen of ours in the opening half.

Trevor played many fine games in his career but if I had to name just one as his best, it was that electric night. He was sheer brilliance. He mesmerised a very good German side, but not only ran the game – he also scored twice! Robbo made it 3–0 by the interval with a typical 25-yard rocket with that left stick, one of the best in the business.

But no German side ever knows when it is beaten. Eintracht threw everything at us after the restart, turning the pattern of play upside down with ten corners against our two. They scored to make it 4–3 on aggregate, and another one would have seen them through on away goals. Despite several scares, however, they didn't get it. West Ham were in a European final.

When they won the trophy eleven seasons earlier, Hammers had the advantage of a 'home' final at Wembley. This time the position was reversed. The final was in Brussels . . . and actually on the home ground of our opponents Anderlecht at their Heysel Stadium headquarters, which has since gained such a tragic notoriety. For us it was very much like playing Liverpool in the FA Cup final – at Anfield!

It should have been the high point of my life, leading Hammers in a European final. Unhappily it was – and remains – clouded by a very sad family tragedy. About three weeks before the final Lyn's mum was taken into hospital seriously ill. In such circumstances, football naturally wasn't the first thing on my mind.

Obviously, I did not want to go away and leave Lyn, and there was a lot of talk at home about whether or not I should play in the final. Lyn's mum was a lovely lady and we'd always got on very well. But both Lyn and her dad insisted I must go to Brussels. 'You cannot do any good staying at home – go and play,' they told me.

In the end I did. But I did not travel with the team when they went out on the Monday before the game. I stayed with the family and flew out on the day of the match with the Supporters' Club on a plane from Luton.

Usually when you are with fans like that the time is spent signing autographs and talking about the club and matches. But those on the plane were aware of my family worry and were very good, just having a brief 'hallo, Billy' chat and then leaving me quietly on my own.

None of it was the best preparation for such a big game, of course. Really all I wanted to do was get out there, play the game, win, lose or draw, and return to Lyn and her dad as quickly as possible.

As far as the actual match was concerned, it began as if we were at home, not the Belgians. We played very well against opponents who seemed to be feeling the pressure of having to do well in front of their own fans. Patsy gave us a deserved lead and Trev was desperately unlucky not to make it two with a volley which rocked the bar. For around forty minutes it looked very much as if the trophy was going to have Hammers' name on it for a second time.

Close to half-time everything changed, Frankie damaged a groin in going to make a run-of-the-mill back-pass. The underhit ball let Anderlecht in for an equaliser right against the run of play.

It was a turning-point. They came out after the interval to slaughter us as Rensenbrink, Arie Hann and Francois Van der Elst played to their brilliant best. They were soon 3–1 up and, though Robbo got one back, it ended 4–2 to them. We could have no complaints; the better side on the night won.

A reception was held after the final, but I did not go. I was booked on a return flight with the Supporters' Club straight away and had to hurry to get changed and join their coach for the airport. I remember several of the lads' wives coming up to me and Fester's wife Greer asking me to give Lyn her love and wish her mum well.

I got home in the small hours of the next morning. I saw at once that Lyn had been crying. She told me her mum had passed away the night before.

Instead of showing Lyn my medal I quietly put it away in a cupboard and it was months later before she even saw it.

22

In 1980–81 our second European campaign, again in the Cup Winners' Cup, had hardly started before I met trouble of a different kind.

The first tie paired us with Castilla, who are virtually a nursery club for Real Madrid. The whole trip turned out to be a nightmare for me! For a start, we'd hardly arrived in Spain before I was hit by a stomach bug. It made a change from normal practice – Trevor having to put up with me being sick all night, instead of the other way round. I managed to train with the lads on the Monday evening, but felt utterly drained. The next day I had to stay in bed and it was touch-and-go whether I'd make the game.

It might have been better if I had not! I presented the Spaniards with a gift goal through a bad back-pass. A bit later the Castilla centre-forward shoved an elbow in my face, forcing a tooth clean through my lip. We played well below form and ended up losing 3–1 to opponents we had considered no great problem before the match.

Afterwards we heard there had been quite a bit of trouble between our fans and the Spanish supporters and police, though none of us had noticed anything much going on during the game. Tragically, one young West Ham follower, innocent of any such involvement, was knocked down and killed by a coach. We learned about these unfortunate incidents mainly from the English reporters out there to cover the match.

Deflated and disappointed, we flew home aware that it would need a return to usual form to overcome that two-goal deficit, but still confident it could be done – particularly as Castilla would find our compact headquarters vastly different from the huge Bernebau Stadium of their parent club, Real Madrid.

When we arrived at Heathrow I was staggered to find a television news reporter and crew there – waiting for me! They got hold of me and demanded to know my comments.

'What about? What are you talking about?' I asked, totally bewildered.

'Haven't you seen the papers?' they cried, and promptly shoved under my nose an English daily which screamed across its back page the words 'You scum!'

I still hadn't any idea why they were grilling me. Then I realised it was what I was supposed to have called our supporters whose behaviour in Spain had created such a rumpus. Even then, it did not really sink in. I had never passed any such comment, not even in private. I was annoyed that somebody, somehow, had managed to tie me in with a situation I knew very little about anyway. But I dismissed the attempted interview by simply telling the truth. I had not called anyone scum, and all I knew about what had gone on in Madrid I'd heard second-hand.

But when our team coach pulled in back at Upton Park I was immediately confronted by an angry fan, who wanted to know what I meant by making such a critical comment on my own club's followers. I assured him that I had not done any such thing and that, until less than an hour before, I'd been completely in the dark about allegedly having done so. And I added for good measure that if he wanted to believe a newspaper instead of me that was his privilege.

We had the following day off, trained on Friday, and played Watford at Upton Park the next day. With no reason to feel guilty, I had by then put the whole business out of my mind. So I was totally unprepared for the reception I got from the terraces when we ran out for the match. For a few moments it just did not register that the crowd were booing me. Then they began chanting, 'We're not scum, Bonzo!' I could not believe the reception they were giving me. I went over to one section of the ground and tried to tell them I'd never said anyone was scum, but they clearly did not want to hear my side of it. Exchanges became increasingly hostile before team-mates pulled me away.

Play started with me seething, badly upset. I'd always had a very good relationship with our crowd. They had known me long enough, and it really hurt that they seemed only too ready to believe something in newspapers which anyone with an ounce of grey matter would not have dreamed of saying. Throughout the ninety minutes parts of the ground kept up almost non-stop barracking. Over the years I'd had plenty of that from opposition fans – but never before from our own.

When I left the ground after the match in my car there were about a dozen people waiting at the exit to give me a further unpleasant dose of their views. West Ham had won 3–2, but I was in no mood for further attempts to justify myself with them over something I had not done, and I just drove past them. It's no good denying I was furious – at the mischief the reports had done, but even more with fans who, it seemed, would so easily turn against me.

By Monday morning I was even more angry. The 'hate' mail began to flood in. Some of it was unbelievably nasty – the worst of it anonymous. I tore them up. But understandably Lyn was very worried.

We had a midweek game at my old club, Charlton, and she tried hard to dissuade me from playing in it. I thought: 'Why should I put my family through this kind of worry? What have I or they done to deserve it?'

But it's not me to run away from any situation. 'I have two options,' I told Lyn. 'I can leave West Ham and play for somebody else, or I can just get on with it, ignore the boos and jeers, and carry on trying to do my best as before.'

I can think of a few players I've known who would have said to themselves: 'What the hell?' and quit the club. Yet I wasn't going to. It would take more than a load of nasty letters to intimidate me.

I played in the game at The Valley, where the reaction from the terraces was about half-and-half as far as I was concerned.

A couple of days later, after further thought, I phoned the newspaper that had printed the 'you scum' report. I asked them if they realised what my family had been going through and what it could have done to my career. They explained that, if their story was properly understood, it had never attached that inflammatory remark directly to me.

'Just try telling that to our fans,' I said. I asked them to print an apology on my behalf. They finally did so, but just a couple of lines tucked away somewhere, with nothing like the prominence given to the cause of all my problems.

It was small consolation for me to learn that the reporter whose name was on the original piece had also received his quota of 'hate' mail, too. While I have never been a headline seeker and will, if possible, avoid being interviewed about anything, that is just because of the kind of person I am, not because I have any dislike of the press. They have a job to do, like the rest of us, and theirs at times cannot be too easy. I certainly would not like trying to find a new sensation every day, even from a business as lively as mine can be.

Once that apology, explanation, retraction – call it what you like – appeared, I was content to let the whole thing blow over, as it naturally did in the course of time. But I was interested to notice recently that there are moves afoot in Parliament to pass legislation aimed at ensuring that newspaper apologies of that kind are given prominence equal to that of the offending report.

Nobody is a stronger believer in freedom of speech than me. It is part of what makes countries like ours so preferable to some of those I briefly experienced on our European competition trips. And without a free press I am sure many things which ought to be exposed would be swept under the carpet. Yet when mistakes are made, and individuals and their families suffer, it would be reassuring to know that errors could be put right in similarly eye-catching headlines. Papers might then be even more careful to make sure they are on safe ground with what they print.

There was no argument, however, that some disgraceful things went on in Spain and that West Ham were badly let down by the behaviour of some visiting fans. For the club was heavily fined as a result, and also ordered to stage the return leg against Castilla behind closed doors at Upton Park, so suffering further financial penalty from lost revenue.

This resulted in the lowest-ever gate for an Upton Park first team match – 262! That total included players, officials, groundstaff and the media.

The game was thus played in an eerie silence before empty stands and terraces, completely devoid of the tremendous vocal support which had always proved so valuable to us. In some ways it was much more like playing in a reserve game than an important European competition. But it made no difference to our approach, and by half-time we led 3–0 to be 4–3 ahead on aggregate. Castilla, however, replied after the break and, though Crossie rocked their bar with a header, the most unusual game Upton Park had ever staged went to extra time. David Cross netted twice in this, completing a hat-trick in the last minute, to put us comfortably through.

Obviously, the circumstances surrounding the tie created a lot of media interest and television cameras were present. Watching the highlights on the box later that night, it was quite easy – and interesting – to pick up what was being said out on the field, with no crowd noise to drown out players' shouts and yells. At least, it was for me until Pikey opened our scoring with a tremendous 25-yarder ... and I saw myself on the screen rushing up to congratulate him and heard very clearly my delighted 'What a ******* great goal, Pikey!'

Our opponents in the next round were completely unknown quantities, Politechnica Timisoara, of Rumania. Before the match John constantly impressed on us the importance of building a good lead in the first leg, which was at Upton Park. 'Teams like these can be very dangerous on their own ground,' he warned.

It was hard to believe this when we hammered them 4–0. They seemed completely cowed by playing here, and one or two of them were definitely not too brave on the night. Tonka was among our scorers – along with me – putting away a penalty after missing an earlier one.

And the Rumanians did not endear themselves to us by complaining over just about everything, despite putting up in a Park Lane hotel! The food, the beds, the rooms ... nothing was right for them. Their moaning seemed even more out of order to us when we played the return leg out there.

A provincial capital, Timisoara is not far inside Rumania's borders with Hungary and Yugoslavia. It has few claims to being among the world's most attractive places. The whole time we were there it rained. The drive from the airport to our hotel was really depressing, with the cloud almost at ground level.

The hotel was, to say the least, spartan, with cockroaches scuttling about our rooms. Eating was a joke. The only edible item on the menu was omelette – and the one I got must have been made from a sparrow's egg. One mouthful and it was gone!

Fortunately, our management had done their homework, and we travelled with ample stocks of our own food – steaks, tea-bags, the lot – so nobody went hungry. Experience over the years has taught English clubs the hard way of the dangers of making such trips without giving the closest attention to every detail.

The Rumanians' ground was a big, open place, with not a stand in sight, just banking, more like an amateur club. As I led our side I was surprised to be handed a big bunch of red roses by a young girl standing by the side of the pitch. For a moment, I wondered if they were trying to tell us something.

When play started it was soon obvious a wreath would have been more appropriate. Some of the worst tackling I've ever seen in my career went on, and we quickly discovered that at home Timisoara were nothing like the timid bunch who played at our ground. They got away with things which would never have gone unpunished in England.

Chief hatchet-man was a little left-back, who must have weighed about nine stone in his clothes. He went around tapping everybody and gave Pat Holland some awful stick. And I could not even remember him from the first game!

They hit a post, but we defended very well, and finally lost by the only goal. But if we'd gone behind early on it could have turned out a very difficult game for us, despite the big lead, and we finished the match fully aware of why John had been so insistent upon going there with a healthy cushion.

Trevor had, as usual, gone down with stomach trouble on arrival, but he was pressed into second-half sub service. At that stage, the challenges were blood-curdling on both sides, and I upset the opposition and their 25,000 spectators with a high tackle on the home star. He was their skipper, a right big old lad, and I caught him as he came steaming through the middle.

Immediately, I was surrounded by the entire Timisoara side, all apparently threatening death. It was all sorted out in the end, but I was not the only Hammer pleased to hear the final whistle. Nor the only one glad when our plane left the ground on the journey home.

23

There was no room for any illusions when the quarter-final draw pitted us against Dinamo Tbilisi. The Russians had put out Liverpool in the previous season's European Cup and their team was studded with players whose reputations were well known this side of the Iron Curtain. But when I reflect on it now it seems we still under-estimated them.

One of the big problems you have when preparing to meet opposition from that part of the globe is that you very rarely get the opportunity to spy on them in advance. This was particularly the case for us. The quarter-final was played in early March. With the Russian season shut down for the mid-winter break, Tbilisi had no league programme John Lyall could refer to. And, though they were keeping active with friendly games in the less frozen parts of the USSR, somehow their schedule for these never reached West Ham ears! The best we could do was to pay a visit to the ITV studios in London and watch some film clips of their previous matches with English teams.

These included that visit to Anfield the season before. Tbilisi lost, but only 2–1, and we saw enough to appreciate how they went through in the return leg. They were obviously among the best sides in Europe at that time, if not the best. In Aleksandr Chivadze they had the Russian Footballer of the Year, who earned this honour ahead of Dinamo Kiev winger Oleg Blokhin, who had been named European Footballer of the Year. Seven other players were Russian internationals, including David Kipiani, the star of a very good squad.

Jimmy Neighbour had played in his Spurs days against Russian opposition, and was not slow to tell us just how big a task we faced. But we were not short on confidence. We'd lost only once at home all season – in the opening game of the campaign against Luton – and it was already virtually certain we were on our way back to the First Division. In addition, we had battled through to a League Cup final against Liverpool, which was due ten days after the visit of Tbilisi. Trevor and Dev were playing marvellously in midfield, and Psycho and Sarge knocking-in loads of goals.

It was a full house at Upton Park for the Russians, yet another of those nights when the atmosphere was white hot from the start. Our approach was the same as had proved so successful in earlier rounds – simply to bomb away at the visitors until they cracked under the pressure. Had we known then what we do now, I suspect the tactics would have been much different!

Totally unworried by playing on our cramped ground and so close to a vociferous, partisan crowd, the Tbilisi players were too good to be ruffled by our storming play. Technically brilliant as individuals, well organised team-wise, they stood up firmly to the pressure and allowed us to create our own downfall by catching us on the break with some superb passing and finishing. By half-time we were two down – and acutely aware this was a vastly different kind of game to any we had ever played in before against European opposition.

Their two first-half goals came in the space of eight minutes after we had done most of the pressing for the opening twenty minutes. Crossie raised our hopes with an early second-half reply – but Shengelia ended our interest in the competition with a goal in the next minute and another before the finish.

The return leg in Tbilisi was still to come, but we really had nothing left but pride to play for after conceding such a daunting first-leg lead.

Tbilisi's manager Nodar Achalkatsi deserved full marks for how well he'd done his homework on us. Unlike John Lyall, he had enjoyed the chance of watching Hammers play before they met his team.

Before we went out there for the return we won a home League game against Newcastle and then played Liverpool at Wembley in the League Cup final. With this ending in a 1–1 draw after extra time, we flew to Russia aware that we had a replay with Liverpool still ahead of us.

West Ham hired their own plane for the long trip to Tbilisi, but could do so only on condition it was a machine from Aeroflot, the Russian national airline. Another requisite was that our flight went via Moscow.

When we arrived at Moscow airport they put us in a lounge while the plane and everything on it was thoroughly searched, which took some time. While this was being done we were not allowed to leave that lounge for any reason. After a couple of hours, several of us needed to answer a call of nature quite badly. But they still would not let us out to the toilet. I think it was only when Eddie Baily, our much-travelled chief scout, called their bluff by threatening to relieve himself where he stood, that the Russian airport staff relented. Even then, we were allowed to go out only two at a time ... with beady-eyed staff for company!

Then it began to snow hard, a real blizzard, and it was quickly obvious we were not going anywhere by plane that night. After a further lengthy wait, the whole West Ham party was transferred by coach to a hotel some fifteen minutes away. I took the chance to look through the snow towards the lights of Moscow, so I at least could say I'd glimpsed a city I would have very much liked to see properly.

That coach ride from airport to hotel was something none of us are likely to ever forget. The driver was a lunatic! Despite the blinding snow, already piling up deep in the street, he blasted through it like a bat out of hell. Clinging on to hard seats for dear life, we quickly worked out that the vehicle was fitted with special snow tyres. It had to be, otherwise we would all have ended up off the road, deep in a snow drift.

It was an unnerving introduction to Russia. Just as were the guys we soon spotted, walking around in pairs, in identical trench-coats with the collars turned up. I had not believed it when friends who'd been there talked about these sinister types – but they were there, all right, no question of us having seen too many anti-Eastern bloc films.

The hotel they put us in overnight was adequate, somewhere to get our heads down, even if it wasn't the Ritz.

Next morning we returned to the airport. The runways had been cleared and we were soon heading south to the warmer climes of Georgia. In fact, when we got to the capital, Tbilisi, it was shirt sleeves weather ... plus 10 degrees compared to the minus 10 we'd left behind in Moscow.

The immediate impression was how friendly everyone was –

once they'd got over to us what seemed a very important point for them: that they were Georgians, not Russians.

The coach journey into town to our hotel was nothing like that hair-raising frightener in Moscow – except, that is, for Ollie! For at one point, when the coach was held up in traffic and we were all staring around at everything, Ollie suddenly yelled: 'Hey, look here, there's a dead bloke right next to me!'

We rushed to look out of his window and, sure enough, right alongside was an open lorry with an equally open coffin on the back. In it, just a couple of feet away from the horrified Ollie, was this poor chap, arms crossed on his chest, and a big photo of him displayed at the head of the coffin.

It underlined for us that we were now in a very different part of the world indeed. And it shook young Ollie rigid. As our coach pulled away, he turned open-mouthed, his face paper-white, speechless. I never asked him, but I suspect it was the first corpse our young midfielder had ever seen – certainly the first at such close range!

The hotel was easily the best of the four I experienced behind the 'Curtain', which was a real relief after the others.

While we had no realistic hope of overturning that three-goal first-leg deficit, our approach to the game was far from defeatist.

We knew we had been 'caught' in that first game by opponents whose skills had been carefully concealed from us. Throughout our squad there was a steely determination to show them they would not get away with it a second time.

But Tbilisi, too, very much wanted to win, not merely sit back and protect that big advantage. They had not lost at home for something like two years, and a huge 80,000 crowd packed into the impressive stadium to see their favourites continue this great run.

They were sadly disappointed! John had accurately sussed out their first-leg tactics and marked our cards accordingly. Alvin and I, at centre-backs, were to stay put, and not allow Tbilisi to pull us away so their loaded midfield could burst through into the spaces created if we let ourselves be lured out of position.

We both did just that and it worked a treat. The Georgians could never prise open the room for the kind of lightning breakouts which devastated us at Upton Park. Long before the finish we had effectively quietened that enormous crowd, who proved not unlike one of our own as they reacted restlessly to their team's failure. With three minutes left, Pancho, who'd come on for Sarge in the second-half, totally hushed the entire stadium by getting the only goal of the game. It wasn't enough to alter the overall outcome, but it ended the unbeaten home record Tbilisi were so justly proud of.

Their manager came round to our dressing-room afterwards and, through an interpreter, told us West Ham were the best side his team had ever played in Europe. Compliments of that kind are easy enough when you've just won ... but I think he was one hundred per cent sincere.

Would we have beaten them had we not gone into that first match so much 'in the dark' as to what to expect? I don't know about that, in all honesty, for they were a very, very good side. But it certainly would have been a lot closer.

24

Never since I joined the club have I ever wanted to play for anyone but West Ham United. Admittedly, I am not aware of a stream of enquiries for my services, but even if there had been I would have had no wish to leave Upton Park.

Like most players, however, I occasionally speculated upon what it must be like to wear the red Liverpool shirt and, year after year, go into every match feeling invincible. I found out in the 1980–81 season, when Hammers set up all kinds of records running away with the Second Division championship and returned to where most felt they properly belonged, in the top flight, after a brief three-year 'exile'.

When a decade earlier I jumped at the chance of moving to Upton Park from Charlton, it was not solely because of financial considerations, even though my weekly pay doubled overnight. Players are naturally ambitious to win something. I was no different to the rest in this respect and, with the fine players West Ham had, thought there was every chance of doing so.

But almost every winter after I arrived seemed to be spent struggling against relegation. Only twice did we finish in the top half of Division One and, though the sixth place in 1972–73 equalled the club's previous best-ever final position, we had come uncomfortably close to the big drop only two seasons earlier, when we ended up twentieth – in those days just one spot above relegation.

The FA Cup win in 1975 and European Cup Winners' Cup final the following season – plus those 'glorious failure' League Cup semi-final tussles with Stoke a little earlier – did much to obscure the lack of League progress. But clubs who so regularly flirt with danger are asking for trouble, and we eventually got it in 1977–78 when, with three clubs now getting the chop, another twentieth place was not enough to preserve our prized record of nineteen years in Division One.

The writing was on the wall almost from the start. The season opened with three defeats and from the first fifteen matches we gleaned only ten points (this was before the three points for a win change).

The previous season I missed only one League game, but injury kept me out for the opening ten of the season which was to end in disaster. After that I was sidelined for only three other matches.

The 22 defeats we suffered were only one fewer than the worst-ever total in West Ham history – and when that record was set in 1931–32 the outcome was also relegation to Division Two. Fifteen of those reverses were away from home. But we gave ourselves real problems by finally losing a traditional ability to win at Upton Park, where the seven defeats we collected were just one fewer than the successes gained.

Despite this, there remained the idea that West Ham were too good to go down; that they would come good yet again to prove this, as so often before. Six wins in the final nine games almost got us out of the wood. But the problem lay in our closing match. We had home advantage for this. There was a nasty 'if only', however, for our visitors were Liverpool! We would have preferred an away encounter at a good many places rather than face the champions in such a vital match.

When Liverpool came to us that Saturday in late April, Forest had already deposed them as champions. But the Anfield lads were only a couple of weeks away from an even more glittering prize, their second successive European Cup triumph, which came in early May when they retained the trophy with a Wembley triumph against Bruges. Five days before the Liverpool game, our flickering survival hopes had been brightly fanned by a 2–1 Ayresome Park win over Middlesbrough.

For that crucial final game the Upton Park gates were closed on over 37,000, the vast majority desperately striving to will us on to the victory which would preserve our Division One status. But taking even one point against such star-packed opposition proved beyond us. Liverpool won 2–0.

It left us with 32 points – and while we were losing to Liverpool, Queens Park Rangers, with Phil Parkes in goal, got a goal-less draw at home to Leeds. That was enough to lift them above us with one game still to play. It was no consolation to us that Rangers, minus Phil, crashed to West London rivals Chelsea the following Monday night. The long threatened axe had already fallen. West Ham, the great entertainers, were down.

I can still vividly recall the sick, empty sensation inside me as we sat in the dressing-room after that Liverpool defeat which ended nineteen successive West Ham seasons in Division One. The feeling of failure was awful, and it was easily my worst-ever moment in the game, even worse than when that sending-off looked like costing me a Wembley appearance several seasons earlier.

Yet I later came to realise that going down did West Ham a world of good!

Inevitably, we looked back over the season and thought bitterly of days when points got away which would have made all the difference. We'd done the double over Newcastle and Ipswich. But while only Liverpool, Manchester City and Bristol City had managed the same against us, too many games were lost by a goal. Our scoring troubles were reflected in the final figures, with Derek Hales being top with ten, one more than Pop Robson. Yet if this suggests we were capable defensively it was not so. We were never tight at the back; always vulnerable.

Among those to depart at the end of the season were Halesie and John Radford. Something of a 'stop gap' buy from Arsenal, where he'd been part of a famous striking partnership with Ray Kennedy in the Gunners' double year, Raddy had enjoyed little luck in his brief stay with us, playing thirty games without once finding the net.

With Alan Devonshire already proving one of the best bargains of all time alongside Trevor in midfield, however, we were confident of bouncing straight back the following season.

Dev had been picked up a couple of years before for a £5,000 'song' out of non-League football. I've often wondered how much heart-burn his subsequent success gave to scouts! Shown the door as a kid by Palace (Malcolm Allison, no less!), Dev must have been watched by representatives from almost every League club in the land during his Isthmian League days at Southall, before Eddie Baily snapped him up for West Ham. Just what scouts look for on such missions I don't know. But I needed only to see Dev in his first-ever training session with us to realise he was a bit special.

This was no particular credit to me, either. When Dev arrived that first day as a West Ham pro, my first thought was: 'He looks like he could do with a good dinner!' Pale faced and with a deceptively slight frame, there was little about him to indicate a rare talent.

Once he got out on the training pitch, however, I swiftly forgot all about the apparent under-nourishment. In no time he was running at fully trained, experienced players and going by them as if they weren't there – and at electrifying pace. And when you tried to put the strong challenge in, he either left you tackling air or simply rode it without loss of control or objective.

Old hands like Frankie, Trev and myself exchanged opinions in the changing-room afterwards. None of us could believe that anyone with such ability had been allowed to languish for so long out of the big time. If we'd known just how good Dev was going to prove, I reckon all three of us would have gone down on bended knees and thanked God!

The tragedy for all of us has been, of course, that serious injury eventually stopped him from enjoying to the full his later years. It was one of the saddest blows ever that, just when Dev should have been taking over the Trevor Brooking midfield mantle, he instead had to battle to overcome problems which would have ended most careers.

But in 1978–79, even with England men Brooking and Devonshire running the show, we soon learned we had no divine right to an immediate First Division return. After a sparkling start, perhaps deceptive, we gradually lost ground and finally finished fifth. We could not point to cup distractions, either, suffering the wrong end of giant-killing acts by little Newport and Swindon in the FA and League Cups respectively.

Scoring was no longer a worry. Pop banged in 24 League goals and had strong support from David Cross with 18. Crossie had been signed midway through the relegation season: a much-travelled, old-style striker with a proven goal record who was expected to add a cutting edge in our attack.

At the end of that first season back in Division Two there

was undoubtedly a much greater awareness of how hard it was to climb back up.

John Lyall caused a stir with a clear-out which saw the departure of, among others, Tommy Taylor, Alan Taylor and John McDowell, all of whom had played in the Cup Winners' Cup final four seasons earlier.

Another of the final line-up, Mervyn Day, had already gone during the preceding season. He moved to Orient when John showed he meant business by paying half a million to lure Phil Parkes to Upton Park from Rangers. Merv was to face us three times in '79–80 ... and end up on the losing side on each occasion! He has since, of course, carved out a career with Villa and Leeds, and also gone into business with success.

When as a teenager he forced his way into the West Ham side, displacing Fester, Ron Greenwood declared: 'He will be our goalkeeper for the next ten years.' At the time it was a prediction we all agreed with. With a fine build, he was excellent on crosses, dominating the area, and full of confidence. I remember a brilliant display he gave in his first season to earn us a point at Everton. At last, it seemed, we had a goalkeeper who could instil confidence.

In three seasons Merv missed only one League game. But as the side struggled in the relegation year, his own confidence waned. He was once chipped from the halfway line at Upton Park – ironically against Everton, the team he had so superbly frustrated at Goodison on a better day. As his form suffered, Mervyn was stuck with that Ron Greenwood remark, which some newspaper managed to dredge up every time he made a slip. It was another classic illustration of what a chancey business football can be. In Ron's place I would probably have come up with a similar forecast and, let's face it, Mervyn is still doing well enough with Leeds.

There are so many ifs and buts, though, that I'm convinced now the worst that can happen to a promising youngster is to be burdened with that kind of tag. Alf Ramsey did Martin Peters no favours when he once rated him as 'ten years ahead of his time'. It was pounced on by the media when Martin later lost his England place.

Publicity is life-blood to the game, but can also terminally affect a young player. West Ham had an unhappy experience of this with Ade Coker, a teenage striker of tremendous natural skill and pace but a physique hardly suited to the rigours of the First Division.

The television cameras happened to be at Selhurst Park the day Ade made his first-team debut against Palace. It was a fine autumn afternoon, the pitch firm, the ball light – all factors in his favour. He was also marked on the day by Palace veteran John McCormack. West Ham were on a good little run at the time and won 3–0, with Ade scoring a goal in a sparkling display. This included one little cameo of his ability on the ball when, challenged near the corner flag, he flicked it up and played it in the air three times to get by. Understandably, TV loved it and ran the action replay over and over, along with highly enthusiastic commentary upon this brilliant new Hammer.

From that moment, Ade was a marked man – very tightly marked, too. There were plenty of defenders who were not going to let him make fools of them and, in the heavy mid-season mud, powered in to brush aside the juggling that had so impressed in the good going at Palace. Ade scored three goals in ten outings before his Upton Park days ended.

He might never have made it anyway. But a kid of that age could hardly be blamed for thinking, after all the praise which followed the Selhurst game, that that was all there was to being a player.

Television could still have had its story; but how much more advised and informed it would have been had they sounded just one cautionary note, reminding viewers – and Ade – that the true test of players and teams has to be over a whole season, in all conditions, against every kind of opposition.

25

Bob Stokoe, my old Charlton manager, was fond of saying: 'Give me a good goalkeeper and a good centre-half, and you've got half a chance.'

His point was amply proved when he was manager at Roker, and Sunderland upset the form book by beating Leeds in the Cup final – with Jim Montgomery in goal and Dave Watson at centre-half. Nobody who saw it is ever likely to forget one save Montgomery pulled off to break Leeds' hearts.

John Lyall's readiness to pay a world record fee for a top-class goalkeeper in Phil Parkes gave us the first half of the equation. Alvin 'Stretch' Martin's emergence through West Ham's youth ranks to international status added the second.

Hammers had never really satisfactorily filled the number five spot since the days of Kenny Brown. They had tried hard enough. John Cushley, Alan Stephenson, Bill Green, Tommy Taylor – all players with admirable qualities – had been bought over the years to fill the spot.

None really succeeded. Cush was a rare battler, who'd give blood, but he lacked the inches to win regularly those important high balls. Stevo and Bill were both strong in that department but, being tall, angular men, not so assured on the ground. Tommy was the most talented of the four. But I suspect his basic easy-going, happy nature made him too nice. There was nothing wrong with his stomach for the game, simply that he was fundamentally not a hard man.

Unlike Ken Brown, very much a local lad, Alvin came to us from his native Liverpool where, though a fervent Anfield follower as a kid, he'd first tried to break into the game with their great rivals Everton. The Goodison club, fortunately for us, did not take him on. Alvin came down for a trial with West Ham and was immediately signed as an apprentice by Ron Greenwood.

He was still a teenager when he made his first-team debut in the season we went down. A regular by the sad end of that campaign, he played more than half the games the following season, and his steady progress and obvious potential were among the factors which decided John Lyall on that clear-out of old hands. In the second season down, Alvin missed only two games, was already earning notices as an England possible – and had convinced me he was the best centre-half I'd ever played alongside.

But in his early days he could be a right little rebel at times. He was so full of confidence that he seemed cocky, and he was not then always the easiest lad to try and tell anything. Yet he was a good, quick learner. One night in a League Cup replay at Southend I had a right go at him about something or other. We finished the match none too happy with a goal-less draw, which meant a second replay against opposition who, on paper, we should have comfortably seen off first time. Afterwards in the dressing-room Alvin came over and said: 'You were quite right, Bonzo, I was out of order there.'

With big Eric in goal and Stretch at centre-half West Ham had the pairing which Bob Stokoe set so much store by.

As a team, we had by then benefited from those two seasons of Second Division competition. We knew there were places we would go where it was necessary for us first to meet fire with fire before imposing our football on the opposition.

For some clubs a visit by West Ham was almost a cup tie. Players of the class of Trevor and Dev had not been seen there too often, so it was all the better if the home lads could take such stars out of their stride on the day. Many opponents accepted that they were not going to beat us on football skills, and understandably tried to stick it on us through sheer work-rate and effort.

It had taken us time, perhaps a bit too long, to adapt, but by 1980–81 we had a squad more than capable of matching anyone who tried to unsettle us by putting it about. Ray Stewart had arrived the previous season to stiffen a defence in which the likes of Stretch, Frankie Lampard and myself could already take care of ourselves. In Patsy Holland and Pikey we had invaluable team men who would run and chase all day – and could also play much better than they were often given credit for. Trevor and Dev had contrasting but superb creative abilities, and the close-season signing of Paul Goddard added more skills and firepower in support of Crossie in attack. To lay on the crosses there was little Jimmy Neighbour, another much under-estimated player. Crossie was then starting his fourth season with us – and had become a much better player. It would have been unusual if he had not, because I can't think of anyone who failed to improve after joining West Ham.

But Crossie was an outstanding case. I've heard John Lyall say more than once that he would have been an England striker if he'd come to Upton Park a bit earlier in his career.

When we signed him, midway through the season when we were relegated, I merely thought: 'Well, at least he's someone who has always got his quota of goals wherever he has played, at whatever level.' We'd faced each other often enough in the past and, to me, he had always been what I regarded as a real 'throw-back' number nine – no unnecessary frills, a hard worker and a forward who was never again diving in where it hurts. As an opponent, in fact, I had come to have regular close acquaintance with those sharp Cross elbows! You never took liberties with him, but, equally, he expected to take as much as he handed out, and did so without making a fuss to the ref.

A couple of seasons playing the West Ham way, however, learning just what to expect from Trevor Brooking and Dev, added immensely to David's game. His touch improved vastly and he became even more proficient in screening the ball from opponents and holding things up just long enough to give team-mates time to join him. And his ratio of goals to chances was better than at any time in his career.

The fans at Upton Park loved him. His willingness to close down defenders and give them a hard time probably did as much as anything else to earn him that affectionate 'Psycho' tag. For it takes a bit of doing to put that kind of pressure on powerful opponents who you know will spend much of a game coming in equally hard from behind.

But one thing David was not was mad! He remains among the most intelligent, educated players I've known, able to talk in an informed manner about all kinds of subjects. And as a footballer he always knew exactly what he was doing. Rarely did you ever see him get involved in the kind of rumpus which I, for example, have sometimes figured in.

David was almost as valuable to us in the dressing-room as on the field. His witty, imaginative mind and a keen, if often droll, sense of humour made for few dull moments when he was around. To us, he was never Psycho – always Norman. Albert Walker, our team attendant in those days, mistakenly called him this once and it stuck for ever after.

The 'Norman' stories are numerous, some of them, I regret, hardly repeatable. For him, being a footballer was not simply a matter of playing matches. He delighted in getting something out of all situations if he could and was never happier than when, poker-faced, he'd succeeded in putting one over somebody.

Once, returning by air from some game abroad, we found the baggage area jammed packed with people. It was obvious that we and our bags were not going to be re-united too quickly. Norman, however, got his in no time – by slipping an arm out of his blazer and then buttoning it tightly across his chest. With his empty sleeve flapping conspicuously, he quickly had sympathetic fellow-passengers sorting out his case for him, despite his protests. They were quite upset when he insisted on walking away carrying his case in the hand he'd been hiding!

On another occasion he found himself sitting in the aircraft alongside a traveller not connected with West Ham. This unfortunate person was swiftly informed that it was David's first experience of flying, that he was very nervous, and would it be all right if they held hands during take-off? Our flight became airborne with Norman tightly clutching a total stranger by the hand.

David was similarly ready for a laugh in less exotic situations. We visited Shrewsbury for a League game one season, just before Christmas. David had come by a very large imitation bank-note, the sort joke shops sell. On the Saturday morning before the match he and a couple of mates went for a stroll around that very pleasant town, and stopped off at a small café for coffee. The bill came to under a pound. Straight-faced, David produced his fake note and handed it to the waitress, with apologies for having nothing smaller. The laugh was on him that time, for the lady, probably busy with a Saturday morning rush, did not catch on, and rushed away with his joke money to see if they could change it!

David further enlivened his morning on the way back to our hotel. The main street was lined with happy youngsters, all eagerly awaiting the arrival of Santa Claus on his progress through town. Every hundred yards or so David got them all cheering wildly with an enthusiastic cry of 'Here he comes!'

I suspect Norman was secretly chuffed by that Psycho tag, if only because it was the kind of thing that appealed to his sense of humour.

But he regaled us once with how it rebounded on him on an occasion when he was escorting a lady friend for the first time, taking her for a meal in rural Essex. Doubtless, on that first get-together, Norman was every bit the charming, mannered, urbane gent. Unfortunately for him, as the pair of them walked along the quiet main street in the little town, a grubby urchin of six or seven came along, kicking an old can with scuffed shoes. Catching sight of our hero, this nipper's face lit up and he came out with an enthusiastic, companionable 'Wotcha, Psycho!' Such is fame! How the lady reacted we were left to speculate.

26

The team that raced away with the Second Division championship in 1980–81 was the best West Ham side I played in. Over a season of 42 games I would back that squad to finish higher in the table than any other West Ham side I was part of. While there was nobody of the reputation of the famous World Cup winning trio of Moore, Peters and Hurst, the overall blend was better.

When I first arrived at West Ham they had several outstanding players, even by world class standards. These made excellent individual contributions in different ways every game; but as a team Hammers often disappointed. That mid-sixties line-up was always going to score goals because of the emphasis upon attacking play, nurtured by Ron Greenwood. Yet it was equally likely to get into trouble by giving soft goals away.

I can imagine my opinion stirring up a few arguments, particularly among team-mates from my first years with the club, who will quickly point out that my 'best' side was largely setting records against Second Division opposition. The answer to that is they also proved their class with those FA Cup and League Cup successes in which some of the best First Division sides of the day were vanquished. I played in both the sixties and the eighties sides and, if I had to make a choice, it would be the latter I'd play in.

One talent we had to do without in that Second Division championship year was Ollie – Paul Allen. After his glorious finish to the previous season with the Wembley win over Arsenal, he was sidelined for almost all the next campaign through injury.

But the side was so strong that his absence was more than adequately covered, even when the unlucky Pat Holland collected a mid-season knock, in scoring a vital goal, which virtually ended his career. Injuries, or rather the lack of them, were another important factor that happy season. Big Eric and Pikey played every League game, and Tonka, Stretch, Norman and I missed only one each.

Ironically, for a side that went on to set all kinds of club records, the season opened with a 2–1 defeat by Luton at Upton Park. It was the only time we lost at home all season in the League. Luton also beat us in the return at their place the following November, and so inflicted the only double that was registered over us – not bad going by the Hatters, considering we lost just four games in all!

Both Luton matches were excellent, particularly the Kenilworth Road one in which we came back from two down to two-all before they nicked it. In recent seasons Luton have attracted criticism because of their plastic pitch, but they have always been opposition I enjoy facing and I can't remember ever being involved in a bad game with them.

Two away draws followed that opening game reverse, so that after three games we had just two points – hardly championship potential. But this undistinguished start was forgotten as we put together sixteen successive home wins.

In fact, we dropped only one more home point all season. That came in March against Oldham, immediately after that long gruelling trip to Tbilisi in the Cup Winners' Cup. The tremendous pace we'd set was just beginning to tell, anyway, and what with the fatigue of such an exhausting midweek excursion we had, as I recall, quite a job holding an Oldham side who played very well on the day to get a 1–1 draw.

By then, however, we had got firmly into the winning habit. It didn't matter where we went, defeat was just never considered a possibility ... as I said earlier, it was the one period in my entire career when I got some idea of what it must be like to play for Liverpool!

There's no doubt that John Lyall had assembled a very good side. But, just like losing, winning does become very much a habit. Confidence soars with every additional success, until it seems nothing can stop the steamroller. For that was what West Ham became that season, crushing everyone in their path and making difficult games look straightforward.

There was only one real hiccup. At Rangers on Boxing Day we had our one bad day of the winter and lost 3–0.

Even that probably did us a favour. In early January we had to go in successive games to Swansea and Notts County, both teams hot on our heels at the time. Still smarting from that Rangers hiding, we won comfortably at Vetch Field and drew with County. The latter game was the one where Patsy was carried off after a collision with home goalkeeper Avramovic as he scored the goal which ensured a point.

Despite an operation and much hard work, Pat never really got over that bad knock and we lost a player I valued highly. Often an undeserved target for the boo boys at Upton Park, Patsy was always among the first I'd have wanted in any side of mine. He had far more ability than he was ever credited with and, even more important, never hid when the going got tough. He could – and did – run all day, and if you were in trouble on the ball you never needed to look far to see him showing up in support.

He also came up with pretty important goals, too, for someone who was not a prolific scorer. That one at County which resulted in his serious injury, for instance. A 1–0 reverse that day instead of the draw might just have started a wobble for us, coming so soon after the 3–0 Rangers debacle. A little slide then and we might possibly have put our concentration into the League Cup, in which we reached the final, and Europe.

I remember a similarly brave effort to win a very hard cup tie at Port Vale, a game so bruising that even such a rugged defender as John Charles had to go off. As Charlo himself said afterwards: 'They've left me white and blue all over!'

And while every Hammers fan can tell you Sparrer scored both goals to beat Fulham at Wembley in 1975, how many remember that each came from crosses by Patsy?

Five years later I did my best to console Patsy after we'd beaten Arsenal at Wembley and he had been left out of the side. He was near to tears in the hotel before the evening's celebration banquet, but after a chat in his room, Patsy quickly came round and shared the pride of a great success, typical of the one hundred per cent team man he was.

There are a couple of other Pat Holland moments I'll never forget, and neither will he. The first was at Ashton Gate when he got his leg broken by a bad tackle. The ref, who should have known better, ordered Pat to stand up, despite the protests of our physio Rob Jenkins. Pat struggled up, put his damaged limb to the ground, and promptly fell down again! It convinced the ref that perhaps he ought to call for the stretcher – but I remember a furious John Lyall informing the official afterwards he would be hearing from the club's solicitors if it was found needless extra damage had been done to Pat's injury.

Patsy seemed to make a habit of finding trouble in the West Country! On a later occasion, after a midweek visit to Cardiff, he rushed to be first back in the dressing-room after the final whistle, grabbed what he thought was a bottle of orange juice, and took a mighty swig. Coming in behind him, we jumped in with such comments as 'You greedy blighter, Dutch, leave some for the rest of us!' But the joking quickly stopped when Patsy changed colour and yelled, 'My mouth's all burning!' It turned out the bottle he'd been so quick to drink from had been left lying about accidentally by the home club ... and contained some kind of cleaning fluid.

Obviously, it could have been very serious. We all knew that people sometimes top themselves that way. Rob Jenkins rushed Patsy off to hospital, where he had to spend the night after being pumped out. Fortunately, no permanent damage was done to the Holland insides – but, believe me, for a decent while after that little episode the rest of us always had a good look at those after-match bottles before drinking.

Despite the absence of both Ollie and Dutch, and the distractions of a League Cup final and European competition, we had the Second Division title and promotion in the bag with three games still to play in 1981. The Second Division shield was presented to us at Upton Park before our final home game, when Wrexham were the visitors. Doing the honours was Sir Matt Busby. It was another memorable moment for me, leading the lads up to the directors' box at West Ham to get the Shield and medals, cheered by massed fans.

Matt Busby is someone I have always admired, and I got a real kick out of having him shake my hand. As a kid it was The Valley I went to, and Charlton were my team. But like Liverpool with youngsters these days, the Busby Babes were also high in my regard then. Getting the trophy from the man who made that squad so famous was the icing on the cake for me.

27

Those exciting seasons of Wembley appearances, European travels and promotion did much to erase the painful memories of years when we always seemed to be slipping up in cups against teams from lower divisions. You could have put together quite a banner with such dubious 'battle honours' on it: Swindon, Mansfield, Hull, Hereford, Stockport, Newport! The majority of these upsets came under Ron Greenwood's managership, when the attacking philosophy produced West Ham teams which could, on their day, beat the best – yet were also quite capable of just the opposite.

Right or wrong, Ron always insisted on football coming first. This led to some famous victories, like that against-the-odds 1964 FA Cup semi-final triumph at Hillsborough over Manchester United – George Best, Bobby Charlton and all. That was before my time, of course, but there's no denying that for many seasons West Ham were always likely to labour against lower division opposition and sparkle playing the top teams.

One factor in those early round cup exits was the conditions. The third round in January often proves a great leveller because of a difficult top. Pitches like that were all against the West Ham style, which was built around playing from the back through the midfield: a much more complicated game than that adopted by lower division opposition, who usually bypassed the midfield and simply whacked long balls forward to put us under pressure.

I think when John Lyall took over he realised West Ham had a soft centre which needed to be hardened up. While much of John's approach is similar to that of the man he learned such a lot from, Ron Greenwood, he has always built strategy upon being strong at the back and matching teams physically, if the need arises. John demands that the individual battles be won first: once they are, you can start playing your football. He still had his cup problems – like the defeat at Newport. Whatever else, though, the Hammers are no longer regarded as the soft touch they once were.

The one West Ham cup flop remembered above any other has to be the infamous Bloomfield Road disaster against Blackpool in the 1971 third round. That was the tie involving the notorious 'night club' episode which, for a time, threatened to split West Ham apart.

But anyone hoping now to read exclusive revelations about the incident can stop right here! I can add nothing factual to what's already long been known. The first I learned of the affair was, like most of you, when I read it in the papers. On the night before the match, when several Hammers visited that night club, me and my room-mate Harry Redknapp were back at the hotel watching television before turning in, and we imagined everyone else was too.

If West Ham had won the following day, I doubt if the night club scandal would ever have had anything like the impact it did. But we had a nightmare game, and Blackpool's 4–0 win hardly flattered them. Struggling well down Division One at the time, Blackpool were relegated at the end of that season. League form, however, traditionally counts for little in the Cup, especially a tie played in the frozen conditions that existed that day in Blackpool.

It was pretty clear to me right from the start that one or two of us did not fancy it. Yet Blackpool's little inside-forward Tony Green revelled on the hard, skiddy pitch and became the key figure of the game.

The previous October we'd beaten them 2–1 at Upton Park in the League. About a month after the cup tie we returned to Bloomfield Road and took a 1–1 draw. That January afternoon, however, they made us look very bad, and we got the press we deserved afterwards.

A couple of days later came the bombshell that skipper Bobby Moore, who'd endured a particularly undistinguished match by his standards, had been among some Hammers seen at former boxer Brian London's Blackpool club on the night before the tie.

When the truth came out, Ron Greenwood was as angry as I ever saw him, and all for sacking those players involved – including England's captain. There was plenty of talk among the rest of us as the bitter row erupted, but it was a time for keeping heads down and mouths firmly shut.

Ron obviously felt badly let down. He trusted players to behave responsibly, and was not the type of manager to go round knocking on doors checking that people were in their rooms. The fact that one of the players concerned was England's captain and another a big name like Jimmy Greaves did not help. But I never have thought the incident had anything to do with the following day's hiding. The players were wrong to have gone to such a place, but they were not out to booze it up, simply to relax, and there was no way any of them would risk being in a bad condition the next day. And if there were four who went out, there were also seven others who did not. The fact was that none of us played too well on the day. The whole eleven of us let down Ron and our supporters.

As to what is right or wrong for players the night before a match – well, obviously, going to a night club is a mistake, even if you intend only a quiet drink. But I know a lot of players whose Friday night would not be right without having a couple of lagers with their dinner. If that is what it takes to put them in the necessary relaxed frame of mind for the next day, then there's no harm in it, any more than a strict teetotaller like Trevor having three or four Cokes.

When the dust finally settled after Blackpool, the only player to get his cards was Stag – Brian Dear. He could hardly complain if he felt he'd been made the scapegoat to carry the can for more illustrious colleagues. Stag was with West Ham only because Ron had given him a second chance, following an earlier move from Upton Park for spells with Fulham and Millwall.

The rest of us, I think, realised all was forgiven on both sides some time later when Hammers were en route to New York by jumbo-jet for an end-of-season game with Santos. We were invited up to the jumbo's hospitality lounge. Mooro and Greavsie were among the lads who accepted – and before long had got Ron Greenwood up there with them. By the time we landed in New York, it was pretty obvious the three had sunk a few jars and were the best of friends!

28

Five Hammers were involved in that Blackpool episode. Four of them were Mooro, Greavsie, Stag and Rob Jenkins, our physio. But I think a few were surprised when the fifth turned out to be our Bermudan striker Clyde Best. The joke was that 'Big Man', as we called Clyde, never touched strong drink. Orange juice was his favourite. So quite how he came to be dragged along with the others I never figured out.

Ron Greenwood has revealed in his autobiography that the West Ham directors over-ruled him about sacking all five, and only Stag went. But they were all fined pretty stiffly, and Mooro and Greavsie were left out for a couple of matches.

Jimmy packed up at the end of that season. But some of us thought he had plenty of football left in him. When he came to Upton Park, the little striker's best days were behind him. He still had that uncanny goal-sense, however, and on his debut with us at Manchester City he scored twice to underline what a great taker of chances he remained.

Very easy to get along with and excellent company, Jim was a smashing fellow. I am sure he could have gone on getting goals for much longer had he chosen to. But maybe he felt his legs were not what they used to be, and decided it was time to retire and try something else. I cannot imagine for one moment that the Blackpool affair had much influence on his decision to quit playing.

Big Man, in contrast, played every League game the following season which, with seventeen goals, proved to be his best for West Ham.

If ever there was truly a gentle giant it was Clyde Best. That was really his problem as a player. With his huge physique and pace, he should have frightened the life out of defences. But while he did not lack bottle, Clyde was simply too nice an individual. He took that very amiable personality out on the field with him and, really, never fulfilled the great potential he had.

There were a few notable occasions when he did use that powerful build to full advantage. I particularly remember a goal he got at Goodison, running from the halfway line with what looked like half the Everton side hanging round his neck but unable to halt him!

We were not short of big men around that time, but Clyde literally dwarfed everyone else in the dressing-room. He'd weigh in for pre-season training at around sixteen stone, looking a fair ringer for Sonny Liston.

He and I were good mates. It was impossible not to be with such a genuine, likeable guy. But once he was very nearly the death of us both. For some reason I forget now, Clyde picked me up to go training one day. He had recently passed his driving test, and his first car was nothing posh. I met him on the West Ham side of the tunnel and we drove off, making for the Chadwell Heath training ground.

Just past Canning Town fly-over a whacking great articulated lorry suddenly decided, without warning, to do a U-turn right in front of us, slewing round from the inside lane. One moment we were tooling along with the road ahead clear, the next there was the whole length of the lorry across our path.

It would have scared an experienced driver. The newly-licensed Clyde had clearly not met with any situation like it before. For a split-second I thought he was going to drive clean underneath the lorry. But when I looked at him to find out what the heck he was up to, all I saw was the big Bermudan with wild staring eyes, sinking lower and lower in his seat.

Luckily, the lorry completed its turn and roared off in the opposite direction before we hit it. But Clyde had lost control and we bounced merrily along the central reservation barrier a few times before he could stop the car. It was already a bit of an old banger – but it picked up a fair amount of bodywork damage. Needless to say, we arrived at Chadwell pretty shaken up ... and I don't remember accepting too many lifts from Big Man after that!

The most modest of people, Clyde was somewhat embarrassed when Hammers went on one of their tours to the States –

and it was the man from Bermuda who was the big name out there, rather than Mooro or any of our stars.

After a similar jaunt to America, we finished up in his home country, Bermuda, and there he was treated almost like a god. Typically, Clyde took us all home to meet his parents and family. They had this pleasant house just a few yards from a quiet little sandy cove and a vivid blue sea. For a sun-lover like me it seemed like paradise, and I couldn't help asking Clyde what on earth made him exchange that for London's East End. I thought he was barmy!

It also explained the sheer delight Big Man displayed the first time he ever saw snow falling. This was down at Portman Road one season. The rest of us were all a bit fed up at having to play in the conditions, but Clyde almost forgot to join the kick-in before the start as he walked about catching snow-flakes in his huge hands, a broad smile on his face.

29

Despite the background to the Blackpool defeat, they were at least a Division One side on their own ground. Some of our other notable cup croppers did not leave us with that excuse!

One of the most emphatic of that kind was the 3–0 stuffing little Mansfield Town handed us in the 1969 fifth round. There was a lot of snow and bad weather about that season, and the game was put off a couple of times before finally being played on a midweek night in atrocious conditions. These were the same for both sides, of course, but Mansfield adapted far better to slay the giant in fine style.

That was the game where I met up with the man who had put me on the right road years before at Charlton – Jock Basford, who was by then assistant to Mansfield manager Tommy Egglington. Jock had another of my former Valley mates playing for Mansfield then, Ray Keeley.

When we were teenagers, Ray was the one everybody at Charlton was firmly convinced had the brightest future. He was the first of my youth team colleagues to break through into Charlton's first team.

Ray reminded me of that early promise during the Mansfield match when he met a cross with a marvellous first-time volley from outside the area. You knew it was a goal from the moment he hit it.

It was Mansfield's night all right. But despite the disappointment I left reflecting the different paths our careers had taken since we played together as hopefuls at Charlton. Then I had thought, along with everyone else, that Ray was easily the best of our bunch. Yet it's me that's ended up with Cup medals and the rest, and who is still earning a living in the game. There has to be a lot of luck in it, being the right bloke at the right time.

It was brought home to me again a couple of seasons back when we were due to visit Southampton. Out of the blue, I got a letter from Ray telling me he had a decorating business at Poole, just along the south coast, and that he was coming to the game at The Dell and would like to meet for a chat. I got Ray a couple of tickets and before the game we had time to talk over the old days. He was doing nicely with his business, I was happy to learn – but again I could not help pondering just how our lives had worked out, and why it was that I should still be playing First Division football and he was right out of the game.

Even the Mansfield exit was not as shameful as losing to Stockport at their place in the 1972–73 League Cup. We were absolutely diabolical that night – we had to be to lose 2–1 to a Fourth Division club. I still remember some of the comments we got from their fans about being over-paid First Division prima-donnas!

Hereford were other minnows we fell foul of in the FA Cup. In 1972 it was like Cup final day down there as we struggled to get a replay with a goal-less draw. The return had to be played in the afternoon, because government power-saving restrictions did not allow the use of floodlights at that time. Over 42,000 crammed into Upton Park and watched Hurstie net a hat-trick to put Hereford in their place.

A couple of seasons later they were back for a third-round tie, and only a spectacular solo equaliser from Patsy Holland stopped them winning. After our previous experience, we did not relish returning to Hereford, who duly knocked us out 2–1.

Those two meetings with Hereford were also notable for the fact that, in the meantime, their winger Dudley Tyler had come to West Ham and then gone back again. Dudley impressed enough in that 1972 tie for Ron Greenwood to buy him for £25,000. It was remarkable that Dudley should ever have played at all, because he'd undergone a 'hole in the heart' operation as a youngster.

Coming from a tight-knit little community like Hereford, Dudley never could quite understand how different life is in the capital. He was always enquiring why all the lads and their wives did not regularly go out socially, and I suspect he privately thought us a very strange bunch because we did not.

But East London is definitely not Hereford. It did not mean

there was anything wrong with team spirit or that nobody got along with anyone else: simply that we mostly lived too far apart to think about any kind of weekly night out with families.

Dudley was back with Hereford by the time we returned to Edgar Street in 1973–74, and it was hard to begrudge him what must still stand out as one of that club's most glorious days.

We had eight players out with injury for the game, including Bobby Moore. So the privilege of skippering West Ham in a cup defeat by Third Division opposition fell to me! I felt a bit better three days later when we beat Manchester United 2–1 at Upton Park in the League. Again I was captain and got my sixth goal of the season to put us ahead. Sammy McIlroy made it 1–1 ... but Patsy came up with another of those rare but vital goals in the closing minutes.

West Ham's Cup record since those seasons of disappointments has been much better. Apart from twice winning the FA Cup and reaching both a European and a League Cup final, the club has only twice gone out at the first hurdle. One of those exits was against Liverpool; the other was when, as the holders, we were beaten by Wrexham in a second replay – and, significantly, in frozen conditions.

Yet the same period also includes our record FA Cup reverse, that 6–1 hiding in a fourth-round replay at Queens Park Rangers. After a 1–1 draw at Upton Park, the return at Loftus Road began well when Pop Robson gave us the lead. Big Eric was in Rangers' goal then, and that was the only time we beat him on what steadily turned into a disaster.

I glimpsed the other side of the game when, after the match, I walked with John Lyall to where we had left our cars parked. On the way I tried to cheer him up with the usual 'there's always another year' kind of comments. But as John unlocked his car, he looked across the roof of it at me and said, 'Those ******* can lose me my job, Bill.'

If and when the time ever comes for me to think about going into that side of football, it will be moments like that I'll remember rather than the euphoria of Wembley!

30

With jokers like Tony Gale about, I'm not allowed to forget these days that I've had more comebacks than Frank Sinatra. If anyone had told me ten years ago that I'd still be playing in the First Division in the late eighties I would have thought they were crazy. But there were a few others, besides Malcolm Macdonald, who believed Billy Bonds was past playing in the top flight when we returned to Division One in 1981–82.

The prospect held no terrors for me, however, even though I was then in my thirty-fifth year. West Ham had a very good side and I was confident we would more than hold our own. From my own point of view, I felt as strong as ever, could train hard, and the idea of retiring simply never entered my head.

I was still coming home first in the long pre-season training runs, which I always enjoy. But it must have been around then that John Lyall put a 'ringer' in against me in a two-lap race at our Chadwell Heath training ground. These things are all part of the build-up to the start of the season and are taken very seriously, with times carefully noted.

John lined me up against this little kid, who'd just become an apprentice. He was of stocky build, but looked so just out of school that I felt a bit sorry for him. Nobody since I'd been at the club had ever finished in front of me over two laps. So it was a major shock – not least to me – when the lad got home with something like ten metres to spare!

Tony Cottee has since acquired a well-deserved reputation for his speed off the mark over a few yards around goal. That was all in the future then. And what none of us, apart from John Lyall, knew was that TC was also the reigning Essex Schools 880 champ the day I met him for the first time and got left behind. John was so careful not to catch my eye afterwards that I often wondered if he had a few bob on that race!

That first season back in Division One opened without distinction as we drew at home to Brighton. But in the next game we slammed Spurs 4–0 on their own ground in midweek, with Crossie getting all four goals to give Ray Clemence a very unhappy match in his early days at White Hart Lane.

Some reports reckoned we'd had all the luck that night, surviving strong pressure to catch Spurs on the break. But the fact is our homework had been done well. Orders were to keep sticking the ball in behind their back four at every opportunity. We did, and it paid off for us and Crossie just as planned.

We went another seven games unbeaten after that. The first defeat, at Villa, was a 3–2 affair, after Trev had given us an early lead with his first goal of the season. Big Eric was missing through a minor knee op, and Tom McAlister was called in for a rare outing. Tom had played patiently in the reserves as Phil's understudy and obviously wanted to impress. But he had a disappointing day by his own standards and was so utterly shattered at feeling he'd let us down that you had to feel for him.

It's always a danger for anyone who has been playing reserve football for any length of time. Neither that or any amount of hard work in training is anything like the same as actually playing First Division stuff. It's a whole different scene, requiring a level of concentration you just cannot gain otherwise, quite apart from the physical demands.

During the season Hammers signed Belgian international François Van der Elst and Neil Orr, from Scotland. François had played in that Cup Winners' Cup final against us in 1975 and, along with Robbie Rensenbrink, had been responsible for most of the damage. Frankie, as he quickly became known at West Ham, played in three other European finals with Anderlecht after that. But he joined us from New York Cosmos, very anxious to re-establish himself in Europe and add to his 34 Belgian caps. At 27, Frankie was still a terrific little player, with great technical skills, pace and scoring ability.

But, like so many foreign players, I think he found it very hard to adjust to the physical helter-skelter action of the English First Division. Over the years, not too many have managed that adjustment. Ossie Ardiles is the outstanding example of one who has ... and I must admit he surprised me and deserves all credit for the way he has not allowed his great talents to be submerged in our hundred mile an hour game.

Frankie had some notable matches for us. I remember a League Cup hat-trick against Notts County and some other brilliantly taken goals. There were times, though, when he clearly felt at a loss as he tried to fit in. He had not been here a month before playing in an FA Cup tie at Watford which typified just about everything in English football. It was a real bruising battle, with the tackles flying in on all sides, and the little Belgian must have thought he was in World War Three! He did enough with us, however, to win back his international place and went on to score some superb goals for Belgium. Some were seen on our TV, and prompted complaints that Frankie did not play like that for West Ham.

In fact, he probably worked harder in Hammers games. He had to, because here the challenges come all over the place. On the Continent they are quite ready to concede space to you until the last third of the field, and are masters at slowing play down before launching a lightning final strike. This was Frankie's game far more than our hurly-burly.

One problem he did not have was language – Frankie spoke better English than most of us! He was also among the nicest of lads. When we played in a pre-season tournament in Brussels the next year, Frankie invited us round to his home there to meet his wife Graziana and all the family, and we spent a very pleasant day.

That tournament was probably among the best we ever figured in. Besides us, it involved Anderlecht, Frankie's old club, Hadjuk Split from Yugoslavia and another local Belgian side. We avenged that Cup Winners' Cup final defeat by beating Anderlecht 1–0. The final against Split ended goal-less and was decided on penalties. We lost the shoot-out when Frankie blasted his spot-kick over the bar!

31

For two-thirds of that 1981–82 return to Division One I was happy enough with my performance. But then it all came to a very sudden, unexpected halt. In late March I found myself having trouble sleeping, something that never normally bothers me. For about a week I was getting up in the middle of the night, unable to settle. I also felt itchy all over and just couldn't keep still for a minute.

On the Saturday we played Forest at Upton Park ... and I realised then something was very definitely wrong when Justin Fashanu began brushing past me as if I was cotton-wool. Lacking any life or strength, I just could not make a tackle, and felt totally leg-less.

During half-time John Lyall asked what was wrong. 'You just don't look yourself at all,' he said.

I managed to see the game out, though I don't know how, and afterwards we agreed I should have a medical check up. I did so on the Monday – and was told I had hepatitis.

It was definitely the end of my season. I never felt so awful in my life as in the following four or five weeks. Utterly uninterested in everything, I just sat in a chair all day. The spring was coming on, a season I always love, but I couldn't even be bothered to go out in the garden. Though I took plenty of liquids, I was unable to force down more than an occasional boiled egg or some cereal. But I know now I was lucky.

Being in excellent physical condition helped me recover after six weeks or so. It wasn't till then that I began to hear the scare stories – about people who had died from the illness, and others who were never the same again after it!

There were no such lasting effects for me, and I was able to start the following season, when only one mid-term injury limited me to 34 League games.

We improved one place upon the previous winter's final ninth position. In the cup competitions we ended up playing

Manchester United in the third round of the FA Cup and Liverpool in the fifth round of the League Cup in the space of three days ... both away! At Old Trafford we lost 2–0, but at Anfield a goal from Ollie looked like earning a deserved replay until Liverpool got a late winner. The competition had earlier pitted us against Stoke again – and this time we came out 3–2 winners on aggregate.

But there was no argument that the departure of Crossie at the end of the previous season had left a gap in our ranks, which neither Sandy Clark nor David Swindlehurst ever really filled successfully.

The 1983–84 season again saw us finish in the top half of the table. I was in my thirty-eighth year and, though I both started and finished the campaign and played 27 League games altogether, I also reached the conclusion that it was time to call it a day at first-team level.

We lost 2–0 at Southampton late in the season and played so badly that I felt very depressed afterwards. Personally, I had done well enough in the game. But I was aware that it was becoming increasingly hard to keep my concentration ... always the sign that I'm not doing the job properly.

At that stage I was playing in the back four, where the involvement is not as intense as in midfield. Physically, I still felt good, and had no worries about pace or strength, but I knew a little bit of my enthusiasm had ebbed away.

The rest of the weekend I turned it over in my mind. All along one thing I'd been positive about was that I was not going to leave it until someone had to come up to me and say: 'Thanks a lot, Bill, but we feel it's time you packed it in now.'

On the Monday after training I asked John Lyall to stay behind with me in the gym when everyone else had left. Then I told him my feelings. 'Maybe it's time you thought about replacing me in the first team,' I said.

Typically, John appreciated how I felt straight away and agreed. But, what was more important, he also agreed that I should carry on playing at a lower level, passing on my experience and advice to younger players in the reserves – for I had no intention of retiring completely.

I knew there was still plenty I could offer West Ham. I wanted

Back in Division One! Frankie Lampard holds the Second Division championship trophy, awarded after our final home game of the 1980–81 season when, with two matches still to play, we were already sure of the title and promotion. Frank's post-game bath-mates – Trevor Brooking, David Cross, Alvin Martin, me, and Paul Brush.

(*Above left*) No need for the make-up department in this Hammer horror shot of what I looked like after accidentally hitting Alvin Martin's boot with my face in 1980!
(*Above right*) Orient skipper and former Hammer Tommy Taylor solemnly greeted me with 'How, Geronimo' when I went to the middle for the toss-up before our Brisbane Road Cup-tie in 1980 looking like this. The bandage covered a gash over my left eye received when Alvin Martin accidentally kicked me during the previous week's match . . . and was Taylor-made for some typical Tommy comment.

Claire and Katie, in younger days, help dad sit in his favourite armchair.

The mad moment which almost cost me a Wembley Cup final appearance in 1980. West Ham vs. Birmingham at Upton Park on Tuesday, 23 April – a tense encounter with promotion for both clubs much involved. Brum's Archie Gemmell (right) and Hammers' Stuart Pearson get between me and visiting skipper Colin Todd after our flare-up, while a posse of Birmingham lads (left) gang-up on Crossie. Toddie and me both went off . . . leaving me to sweat on a suspension that I feared would stop me leading West Ham out at Wembley soon after.

They reckon he did not score enough goals – but the one Trev got at Wembley in 1980 was sufficient to scupper the Gunners. He headed it, too . . . no wonder we are both so ecstatic.

Not every day you meet a real-life Duchess . . . but I seem to have eyes only for that coveted bauble as the Duchess of Kent hands it to me after our Wembley win over Arsenal.

Our chairman Len Cearns and his wife look on as I do the cup-brandishing ritual after we'd seen off Arsenal – a moment when you truly lose touch with reality.

Castilla captain Jose Castro and I shake hands, watched by French ref Delmer, before the start of the Cup-Winners' Cup match in Madrid's Bernabeu stadium.

Castilla skipper Jose Castro and I lead the sides out for that 'closed doors' Cup-Winners' Cup-tie at Upton Park in 1980.

Standing next to my old guv', England manager Ron Greenwood, in the squad group picture taken at the team's hotel. Ron had me on the subs' bench for the World Cup qualifying win over Italy at Wembley – the nearest I ever got to a cap.

Last of the summer wine! Trevor, me and Frankie pictured during a pre-season training session at Chadwell Heath before the start of Trev's final campaign.

Our chairman Len Cearns makes a dressing-room presentation to me for topping Mooro's record for club league appearances, watched by John Lyall.

Dicko' tries a bit of bluff with that satisfied half-smile as the pair of us examine our hands during a card-school session on the team coach to an away match. But things were not always so well-behaved!

Geronimo rides again! A gashed head during our win over Forest at Upton Park in the 1987–88 season resulted in me once again playing out the match heavily bandaged. Here, I manage to get between Forest's Brian Rice (left) and Terry Wilson.

(*Above left*) Forest chairman Maurice Roworth presented me with this lovely cut-glass vase, inscribed with their crest, after our match at the City Ground in 1987 – a marvellous gesture prompted by the thought it would be my last appearance against Forest. But I faced them twice more the next season . . . and we took four points off Forest!
(*Above right*) Collector's item! Rare picture of yours truly in evening dress, receiving the PFA Merit Award from FA secretary Ted Croker earlier this year.

A day none of the family will ever forget. Claire, Lyn, Katie and I have our picture taken in the courtyard at Buckingham Palace after my MBE award – which Katie is so happy to display.

Coast-to-coast coverage for Billy Bonds, MBE. America's NBC network London man Henry Champ and his camera crew interview me following the MBE award.

to put back into the club as much as I could by doing some coaching if possible and by playing alongside tomorrow's first-teamers in games where I could teach by example and attitude.

Ironically, after that dismal day at The Dell, we next went to Old Trafford and played very well to get a goal-less draw. I was up against Mark Hughes and really enjoyed keeping him out. But though I played out the rest of the season I had made up my mind about stepping down as first-team captain the following winter. With Trevor hanging up his boots it was the end of an era, and it seemed an appropriate moment for me to move off centre-stage, where I had been for seventeen seasons packed with highs and lows.

What I then took to be my final campaign had included both extremes. Among the lows was a single-goal third round FA Cup home win over Wigan which saw Dev collect a desperately serious ligament injury that would have finished many players. I would much rather have lost on the day than have that happen.

After two years of struggle against set-backs and tremendously hard work, Dev came back to play brilliantly in what was to prove West Ham's best-ever season. But he has rarely been free from problems since, and there's no doubt that injury has blighted his later years.

Even the season's high point was a bit tarnished for me. This was the record League Cup 10–0 spree against Bury at Upton Park. Playing in midfield, I got forward for a couple of knock-downs which Tony Cottee latched on to as he plundered four goals. But I never saw out that historic game. The trouble was that the ref, David Letts, is one I have never rated, a view which usually leads me into saying more than I should and going in his book. John Lyall sussed out what was going on between us and yanked me off at half-time to keep me away from real problems.

Having running battles with officials is not my idea of how to carry on. They have an unenviable job to start with, and constant back-chat from players cannot help. By and large I accept that anything I got from refs over the years I deserved. My first sending-off against Hull was an example. Once I cooled down after the match I knew how wrong I'd been to react the way I did. I went to the ref's room and apologised to Norman

Burtenshaw. It was in no way an attempt to get out of anything. I'd gone off and nothing would alter that. Norman Burtenshaw was, I suspect, as upset as I was about the whole business. 'Players who do what you did leave referees no option but to do what I did,' he said. 'I'm glad you realise that, and I hope you never do it again.'

David Letts, however, always seemed to be hard on me – we once had a dust-up in a pre-season friendly! Even in that Bury game he gave a penalty against me that was absurd. He said I climbed all over an opponent heading clear, which I hadn't; and it was outside the box, anyway.

He's a policeman in everyday life, and I'm surprised he's never yet checked my road fund licence on his way home! Maybe he has professional connections with the long-suffering Old Bill who used to be regularly called out to chase us kids away from those 'no ball games' council greens in Eltham!

The worst day of all for Hammers that 1983–84 season came in a later FA Cup tie at Birmingham, which is something of a bogey ground for us. Three down, we had only pride left to play for. But the chance of even that vanished when so-called supporters made a disgraceful second-half pitch invasion which forced the ref to take us off while order was restored. What had gone on out in Spain four seasons before was immediately dredged up again in the media, and West Ham got another panning, although a subsequent FA inquiry cleared the club from any responsibility.

Funnily enough it was during a much later cup tie, with the teams again taken off by the referee, that West Ham's fans must have done the chances of English clubs being allowed back into European competition a power of good.

Doubtless, many reading this will have been among the 10,000-plus Hammers followers who crossed London for last season's FA Cup match at QPR – and more than a few of them involved in the crowd spill-over on to the pitch as a result of too many spectators being allowed into a section of the Loftus Road ground.

With hundreds clustered so close to the lines each side of the goal and down the wings it was obviously impossible for play to continue, and the ref rightly took us off. Galey, Tony Cottee and one or two others went into Rangers' boot room and joined some of their players and groundstaff watching the scores come up on television. After a time, Parkesie, who'd been scrounging tea off his old club-mates, came in and advised us that it was unlikely the game would be resumed.

A quick look out of the tunnel confirmed this view. Both managers, John Lyall and Jim Smith, Hammers secretary Tom Finn, and umpteen stewards and police were still striving to fit the overflowing fans back on to the terraces.

It was an extremely volatile situation. A very large West Ham contingent had paid their money to get in. Many of them had endured what must have been shocking discomfort in that over-full area, and can have hardly seen much of the play before the stoppage. Now it looked as if they were not going to see any more at all on the day.

All the ingredients were there for a right old flare-up. You could already see the headlines: West Ham hooligans at it again. But to their great credit, those hundreds of 'displaced' supporters put up with all the marching about from one part of the ground to another, the orders and counter-orders, the confusion, with real old-fashioned Cockney good humour.

Some of them may have read in the papers before the tie that half-a-dozen top brass from the West German police were coming to the match, especially to see how our police operated and to liaise over plans for the summer's European Championships finals in West Germany. Some of them . . . but not all. Yet if you had pleaded with those mucked-about fans to show the foreign visitors the best side of the British character they could hardly have done more to oblige. In an almost frightening situation which called for much tact, diplomacy and hard work from the police, they received total co-operation from the supporters of West Ham United. From an apparently hopeless, out of control position, order was slowly but surely restored, and the game restarted after almost exactly an hour's delay.

It must have enormously impressed those watching German cops. The story they took back home can have done nothing but good for the prospects of that Euro ban being lifted . . . and, if and when it is, then the supporters of West Ham United who were at QPR that day can certainly pat themselves on the back.

32

After nearly two decades with the club it was rich irony that in the one season when West Ham really did have a championship chance I never kicked a ball at first-team level!

While Hammers had the big boys looking anxiously over their shoulders my only concern was getting over a problem well enough to lead a normal life, let alone play again. It was all the more galling to miss the entire 1985–86 season because in the previous one I had twice been called up out of the reserves where, following my decision to step down as club captain, I expected to play out the rest of my career.

That 'retirement', in fact, lasted just one day.

The 1984–85 campaign started for me in the reserves at Bristol Rovers. The following day I got a phone call telling me to report for the Sunday trip to play Liverpool on the Bank Holiday Monday. The immediate comeback also set the pattern for others in later seasons. One came at Forest and another at Everton ... three returns very much in the deep end! After the Liverpool game, which we lost 3–0, I had twelve more outings before being sidelined with knee ligament damage resulting from a bad tackle from behind by Albion's Tony Grealish at Upton Park.

At my time of life it was an injury which might well have persuaded me to pack it in altogether. It's a lot harder to get over knocks like that as a veteran and, though I still found playing First Division football no problem, getting out of bed the next day invariably reminded me my fortieth birthday was coming up!

But I was recalled for the second time that season to play another seven games late in the programme. The final match, at home to Liverpool, threatened for a time to be a repeat of the 1977–78 relegation year, with us having to win to stay up. In the end, however, we had ensured safety before then, and I did not play that closing game.

Obviously, I hardly saw myself as being around the first team the following season, short of a really bad spate of injuries to others. So what looked very likely to be my own final home first-team appearance came in the game before Liverpool's visit, when we beat Stoke 5–2. I scored twice to make it a nice farewell to the big time – or so I thought.

This seemed even more certain when, before the start of the next season, my sole concern was a problem which had me seriously worried about ever being able to lead a normal life again. Playing, at any level, was just about the last consideration.

For some time I'd had recurring troubles with the little toe on my right foot. As long as I could remember a soft corn between the toes had required regular attention. Now infection had set in. A course of strong anti-biotics failed to work and, with the infection attacking the bone, an operation was necessary. This was done in August, but almost at once I was aware it had succeeded no better than the drugs.

After the various, often quite serious knocks I'd overcome during the years, it was almost funny that something like a little toe should be more painful than anything I had previously encountered. But it was no joke for me. For months it was completely impossible to wear any kind of shoe, and I went around in flip-flops simply to keep the pressure off the toe. The pain was so severe that amputation became a serious possibility.

In my fortieth year I really could have few complaints if my playing days were over. But it was not having to quit that worried me. I just wanted something done so I would be able to walk normally for the rest of my life!

Once again, West Ham's surgeon Brian Roper stepped in to use his skills and give me another lease of playing life. He performed a second operation in November, and this was a total success. For the second time Brian had extended a career that looked finished.

Recovery was a slow, painful business. But I at least had the great satisfaction of watching West Ham play marvellously. John Lyall had brought in Mark Ward and Frank McAvennie, and both performed far better than anyone could have hoped. Dev was back, as good as ever, totally disproving those who'd written him off, after that bad injury, by playing 38 League games, which was a tribute to the hard work he'd put in.

It was a choker for me not being part of that squad, after so many seasons of struggle. With Frank having only to be in the area to score, the side played confident, positive one- and two-touch football, using the ball quick and early in such a way that the opposition had no counter. I would have loved the chance to play in that set-up.

Yet, if I was disappointed not to, I certainly was never bitter. After all, even if I'd been fully fit, where would I have got in? We could have had better players than me on the sidelines at that time to whom the same would have applied – Sarge, for instance, had the bad luck to be injured in the opening game and never could regain a regular place. The team was virtually free from injury, too, throughout the season, and John Lyall naturally would not have wanted to change such a successful line-up.

I watched more games that year than I'd seen in the past twenty, I reckon. Normally I am a poor spectator. If I'm not involved out there I rarely enjoy looking on. But if I couldn't play, then watching was the next best thing during that great season.

Sixth place was the best any side I'd played in had managed, and then there had never been any realistic title involvement. But this time West Ham really were in with a shout. Just how convinced I was of this is shown by the fact that I put £50 on them at eight to one to finish champions. I like a bet, but that was far more than I would ever put on a horse or dog.

Finally, a backlog of fixtures resulted in cramming the last ten games into less than thirty days. Eight of the first nine were won despite the almost non-stop action, but a 2–1 home slip against Chelsea eventually proved crucial, although it was not until the last Saturday of the season, when Liverpool won at Stamford Bridge, that the championship went to Anfield.

There were several stars for West Ham in that year, not least new boys McAvennie and Ward. But to me the real reason for success was that everyone regularly played to their full potential at the same time, largely as a result of the confidence which flowed through the side more and more the longer it went on winning.

33

The only two incidents involving club-mates I have had were both, by an odd coincidence, with players who'd been Manchester United centre-forwards! Neither bust-up got to the brawling stage, although the first, with Ted MacDougall, would certainly have done so as far as I was concerned, but for Ron Greenwood. MacDougall put it about in the press later that we'd actually had a fight, and he'd got the first punch in. That was typical of the man.

From the moment he joined us after his spell with Tommy Docherty's Manchester United, trouble between him and me was inevitable. There was an immediate oil-and-water personality clash. His arrogant attitude got under my skin, particularly when he behaved that way towards hotel and restaurant staff. I played with and against some really great strikers, far better than he ever was. Yet none of them carried on as if waiters, receptionists and the like were just menial workers instead of ordinary, decent people doing a job.

As a player MacDougall had very definite limitations. Teams naturally always try to play to particular individual strengths. With him, this left few options.

He'd played only a handful of games with us when our flare-up came. It followed a 4–1 defeat at Leeds. During the game I had not been impressed with his work-rate. He clearly considered the service we provided was not up to the mark. No doubt there was something in each point of view. At the finish some angry words passed between us in the tunnel. Then, soon after, when I was in the bath and still simmering, MacDougall came in and the row started up again.

Ron Greenwood heard the slanging match and rushed in from the dressing-room to get between us just before it got really serious. He ordered us both to calm down, pushed MacDougall back into the dressing-room, and left me sitting in the bath. The manager was the only one to suffer any real damage out of it –

ending up with a pretty damp suit from the water that had come with me as I clambered out of the bath!

Neither of us were disciplined over the bust-up. But MacDougall was soon putting it about he would not be at West Ham long after that incident, because I was Ron Greenwood's favourite. Well, he was right about not staying long. Before the following season was half over, he continued his wanderings by joining Norwich.

I may well have been a Greenwood favourite but, if so, that had far less to do with MacDougall's departure than did the repetition of the lack of goals which led to him leaving Old Trafford.

Just a month after he went from West Ham he was back at Upton Park with Norwich, giving us a quick chance to settle the score. And I admit I went into that match resolved that, if the ball and MacDougall were there, I would not hold back in the tackle.

There was a crowd of over 32,000. The vast majority, it seemed, having read MacDougall's much-publicised bragging in the press about what he called our 'fight', were there mainly to see what I was going to do about it. I got plenty of advice from the terraces.

But, like the flare-up itself, it all finally came to nothing. My approach to the action was not lost upon our bench ... and before long I received a firm instruction to move out of midfield and play out the rest of the game at centre-forward, away from possible punch-up problems!

The second barney was with Pancho – Stuart Pearson. Like MacDougall, he joined West Ham after leading the Manchester United attack, but with considerably greater skill and distincition. There was no doubting Pancho's talents. He had England caps to prove them.

Pancho and I never had a lot to say to each other, but that's nothing out of the ordinary in football. Some team-mates you chat to a lot, while others, without being unfriendly, are content just to pass the time of day.

Birmingham's St Andrew's ground was rarely a good one for us, and in one 3–0 defeat there I had a go at Pancho, among others, for not doing enough. He took great exception to this, apparently because he thought I called him a cheat.

We happened to be close to each other when the whistle went and, going down the tunnel, Pancho made a few choice comments to me. Coming on top of the stuffing we'd just taken, it was more than enough to start up a right row between us. The Brum lads must have chuckled to themselves as they passed the pair of us mouthing off at each other, being restrained by team-mates.

It did not go beyond that. Fortunately, unlike MacDougall, Pancho did not leave. Though injury problems limited his appearances for West Ham, he remained to play a vital part in the defeat of Arsenal in that Wembley final.

That was really his scene: the big game, the big occasion. Perhaps it stemmed from the years he enjoyed responding to the applause of that tremendous Old Trafford following.

'Fights' in football are almost always something of a joke, really, with the verbal exchanges far harder than any swapped punches. But I vividly recall one where the reverse, for once, was true . . . and again it was between club-mates!

During training one day John McDowell succeeded in really winding-up his West Ham full-back partner Frankie Lampard. John was a good defender and very capably took my place at full-back when I switched to a midfield role. He was never a bad lad at all, but he did have one fault – too much to say. On the occasion in question it was this which had got to Frank, who advised him to keep his trap shut . . . or else. The warning went unheeded, and the pair finally ended up in an eyeball-to-eyeball confrontation. Unwisely, John thrust his chin out and dared Frankie: 'Go on then, put it there!' Which is exactly what Frank did without further ado!

John trailed away to the dressing-room, nose streaming blood, definitely a sadder if not wiser man. Frank was duly fined pretty stiffly by John Lyall, but seemed to think it was worth it!

Even that most mild-tempered of men, Trevor Brooking, lost his cool with John on another occasion. Trevor was among four of us playing cards on a train going home after some game. John knelt on his own seat so he could look over Trev's shoulder and, as usual, was not slow with the advice on how to play the hands. After several vain requests to be left to make his own decisions about this, the Brooking patience snapped, and he turned round and whacked John across the top of his head, giving him a most un-Brooking like volley.

'What's the matter with him, then?' complained John, as he sank back in his seat, clearly baffled that he could possibly have upset anyone.

He suffered similarly another time during a pre-season tour in Norway. We were having a quiet drink in our hotel one evening, and John had a go about something or other at Graham Paddon, who, to me, was one of the best left-side midfield men I ever played alongside.

Graham was a cool, laid-back type, slow to anger in any situation. He stood there, with a glass of lager in his hand, letting John run on for a few moments. Then he walked over to him and poured the whole glass over John's head. Graham walked away without a word, leaving an astonished – and very wet – John McDowell speechless for once!

John had another little habit which did not exactly make him Mr Popular with the card school regulars. He would occasionally join in and, if he got a few quid up, get out again – definitely not done.

But if John was not too welcome at cards, there were a couple of others who always were: Neil Orr and Sandy Clark. It was a sad day for the rest of the card school when that pair returned to Scotland. Both were very bright lads – Neil did an electronics evening course while he was with us, and Sandy had previously managed a finance company office. But they were hopeless at cards. We knew we were good for some winnings by the end of the trip if they came in.

One of our favourite games is 'hearts', with the stakes a penny a point, so you can see the stakes were rarely very high. I got stung only once. Bill Green wanted to play one day and borrowed off me to do so. He lost, and said he'd pay me back the following Monday. But the jolly Green giant, as Tommy Taylor dubbed him, was eventually transferred from West Ham still owing me.

I wrote it down to experience. But a few years later West Ham played at Watford one Saturday and, instead of the usual hotel, we went to some little place out in the sticks for the pre-match meal. As soon as I walked through the front door the first person I saw was Bill, sitting just inside reading a paper. He was then with Chesterfield, who must have been down south playing in the same area.

I don't know which of us was the more embarrassed by the unexpected meeting. It was obvious to both of us that neither had forgotten that outstanding debt. Yet it wasn't mentioned. We just said 'Hello, Bill' and 'Hello, Bill' and 'All the best today', and that was that. It still is, too!

34

If anyone ever had reason to be doubly delighted with the arrival of his children it has to be me ... because on both occasions West Ham went on to win the next FA Cup final! Our first daughter, Claire, was born in November 1974, and Hammers beat Fulham at Wembley the following May. Katie was born in May 1979, and a year later West Ham again won the Cup, defeating Arsenal. I've wondered a few times since if Lyn and I ought to go for the hat-trick!

After Claire was born I was on such a high that I followed a virtually sleepless night with a train journey to the other end of the country and then played ninety minutes of First Division action without the slightest problem.

Lyn went into hospital early to have Claire. We had agreed I would be there, so I was in and out of the hospital all week. On the Friday I was assured nothing was going to happen for a couple of days, so I left and drove up to Euston to join the team on the way to Carlisle. But no sooner had I got to Euston than a loudspeaker announcement called me to the station office, where I was handed a scribbled message asking me to return at once to the hospital. That crumpled piece of paper is still among our treasured possessions.

While West Ham travelled north without me, I did a Stirling Moss through the traffic back the way I had just come, praying the baby would wait until I arrived at the hospital. When I got there, of course, the nursing staff told me to go away again – there was not that much of a hurry!

Nerves jangling, I went to a pub for some lunch. But I was on such tenterhooks, and they took so long coming for my order, that I rushed out and found another pub closer to the hospital. Appetite gone, I had half a shandy and some peanuts before tearing back to see if anything was happening.

Claire arrived at five to eleven that night – the most marvellous experience of my life being present for her first look at the world.

By the time our new little girl and Lyn were sleeping soundly, and I'd phoned the news all round the family and friends, it was close on two in the morning when I finally got back home. I was still so excited that getting any worthwhile shut-eye in what was left of the night was impossible.

Next morning, on top of the world, I drove up to Euston once more and caught the early train to Carlisle. That trip passes some lovely country and I would have enjoyed it at any time. Being a proud new dad made it even better.

It was cheers and congratulations on all sides when I joined the rest of the lads at the hotel in Carlisle. The game was played in the kind of difficult wind you always seem to get in those parts. I remember little about it, except that we won 1–0 with a Frankie Lampard goal.

That was Carlisle's only season in the top flight, defeat on the day pushing them closer to the relegation which came at the end of the campaign. But while I was happily relaxing in the bath after the match, their chairman Mr Sheffield walked in and presented me with a bottle of bubbly and congratulated me on becoming a dad – a smashing gesture and typical of that homely club.

Claire was six months old when we went to Wembley the following May, and before the final there were pictures in the papers of me holding her in my arms in the back garden. I was even more proud then than when I received the MBE.

When Katie was born three and a bit years later it was altogether different from Claire's arrival. Katie came just after the season ended, about twenty to one on a Saturday afternoon. Once we knew everything was fine I rushed round to my parents to tell them we had another girl. Mum was thrilled to bits, but I remember Dad was glued to the England v Scotland game at Wembley on the box and just about managed to glance up and say, 'Well done, lad!'

At the time it certainly never crossed my mind that, as with Claire, Katie's birth would be followed by our own trip to Wembley. But it was, and I have the great good fortune to possess two FA Cup final winner's medals. At some suitable moment in the future I plan to have them mounted and give one each to Claire and Katie. It could lead to a slight rumpus! For some reason, the Fulham gold medal is much less shiny than the Arsenal one. If that starts an argument over who has what, I'll just have to be the firm father for once!

35

Players always eagerly seize upon the chance of a celebration when a team-mate becomes a dad. One I'll never forget was when Peter 'Les' Bennett's first nipper was born . . . because he came uncomfortably close to never seeing his offspring!

Just as Mrs B was about due to enter hospital, Les left with the rest of us on a six-week summer tour of America.

That was the trip where we played English and Scottish opposition in a league, home and away, each team based in a different city. West Ham were quartered in Baltimore, and we covered thousands of miles going to play in places like Dallas, Kansas, Seattle and Portland.

When Les got the news that he was a dad for the first time, we went out that night to celebrate in a restaurant across the street from our motel. Baby Bennett's head was well and truly wetted, believe me. It turned out to be a unique occasion, too, for it was the one and only time we ever persuaded Trevor Brooking to touch alcohol!

It was pretty late when we returned to our motel – Trevor apart, all happily stoned. Harry Redknapp, Trevor, Jimmy Lindsay and I suddenly got the idea of giving Les a fitting end to the celebration by chucking him into the motel swimming pool. He was in no fit state to argue, so we heaved him in with a mighty splash, stood back laughing like mad, and waited for the proud new dad to crawl out.

But none of us had quite realised just how blotto Les was. Instead of surfacing, spluttering and cursing, he simply lay quietly floating face down on the water, arms and legs gracefully spreadeagled. Panic set in as he did not move. There was only one answer, and a couple of us had to jump in and haul him back on to dry land before it was too late. The 'rescue' sobered us all up pretty quickly, and we trailed off to bed much wetter outside than we were in!

Les is among the many smashing blokes I've met in football.

After he left Hammers we had no real contact. But when I resumed playing, after that whole season out with the toe problem, I suddenly got a Christmas card from him, saying how pleased he was I had recovered enough to keep playing. It really bucked me to hear from someone who'd been a team-mate all those years before, and who took the time and trouble to send a card like that. That kind of keeping in touch is one of the really nice spin-offs in football.

In his West Ham days Les was a fully paid-up member of a card school still notorious for cheating, along with Harry, Trevor, Jimmy, Ronnie Boyce and me. Bigger cheats there never were! It got so bad that, finally, we had to do something, and brought in a spot-check system in which anyone could demand to see the cards of a suspected twister. This worked well enough until one day, on a train journey home from an away game somewhere, Les wanted to look at Harry's hand. Harry was always a slippery customer – so much so, in fact, that we called him The Fox.

But he would not have it this time. 'If you won't take my word for it I'm not cheating, I'll sling the cards out of the window,' he raged. Les wouldn't; Harry did ... and we spent the rest of the trip sitting there in a temper without any cards at all!

Apart from nearly bringing the Les Bennett career to a premature end, Harry Redknapp and I had other reasons to remember that long jaunt in the States.

Lyn and I were all set to be married on my return. Before I went, she specifically warned me about taking too much sun. 'Just don't you come back black and spoil the wedding photographs,' she said. But for a sun-worshipper it was impossible, with temperatures in some places around a hundred in the shade. It was equally tricky for Harry, who was my Best Man and who, like most red-haired people, simply turns a bright puce in the sun.

I've never lived those wedding group pictures down with Lyn! There's H looking like a lobster, while all you can see of the bridegroom, black as the ace of spades, is a pair of white eyes shining like the proverbial sweep's tanner!

On our big day H never helped much either by keeping his

hands shoved in his pockets. Every picture he's in, there's the rest of us putting on the style and H standing there with his maulers in his trouser pockets. Even when he had to get the ring out of his top pocket, he kept his other hand firmly on his small change. Brown boots, I ask yer!

It's a pity he is not still at West Ham. J. Lyall is hot stuff on the 50p fines for hands in pockets – it would cost H a fortune.

We were great mates in those days, playing together down the right side of the field and always sharing a room on away trips.

H was a match-winner on his day and, though he was inconsistent, became the favourite of a West Ham crowd who traditionally had flying wingers to roar on right from early post-war years ... Eric Parsons, Terry Woodgate, Harry Hooper and Mike Grice.

H had a lot of pace and ability – not to mention that red hair – and the chicken-run regulars used to go potty if ever a defender had him over in full flight.

As an attacking right-back, I was always up in support, and so on those frequent occasions it was me who charged up to sort out the offender. It became accepted practice that I would fight Harry's battles. But when he got his one sending-off, up at Leeds, Billy Bremner really kippered the lot of us.

Whenever we met Leeds, Ron Greenwood always demanded that H and me got at Terry Cooper, then England's left-back, who Ron reckoned was great going forward but could be exposed if attacked. I wouldn't argue with Ron's view – but we never found out if he was right. Against such a fine winger as Eddie Gray I always had more than enough on my hands without thinking about putting Cooper under pressure. And H spent most of his time chasing back to help out as the Leeds lads queued up to take me on.

In the game when H got an early bath he'd been niggling all through with Bremner, a terrific little player but also full of the tricks of the trade. We got a corner on the left and, as this was taken, Bremner suddenly went down as if pole-axed in his own area.

It was a joke. H never stuck one on anyone in his life – and if he tried his hardest could not have flattened Bremner the way the Leeds star dropped. The idea is about as daft as putting Tony Cottee in with Tyson. But despite our outraged protests, the ref bought it, H went, and we ended up with ten men!

H and I had our little successes, though. One lad we always loved playing against was John Winfield, the tall Forest defender. We regularly gave him a chasing with one-twos down the right and by playing little short balls between us all around him.

Close as we were, H and I had one notable falling-out. He always put my bets on for me, and one Saturday we were up north for a game. For some reason, H was not with us, and when I spotted a ten to one shot I really fancied, I got on the phone and told him to put a fiver on – a big bet for me even now.

The race was on the box in our hotel and I watched my nag soar home. Fifty quid, plus my fiver back – the best win I'd ever had!

I got straight back on the phone to H, all excited . . . only for him to reveal he'd been unable to place the bet. He reckoned the line was engaged. We had a right barney over it and didn't talk to each other for all of a week. To this day he swears he couldn't get through to the bookie. I'm still positive he stuck my fiver!

H was one of those many players who have to be sick before a game. You'd go into the toilet and find him with his fingers down his gullet, trying to throw up. It's part of getting psyched up for the action, just as there are others who have to pay half-a-dozen visits to the loo. Tony Gale is like H: he just does not feel right if he has to go out and play on anything but an empty stomach, even though he's hardly eaten anything, anyway. Whatever might be in there has to come out.

I confess I'm surprised H is now doing such a good job as manager at Bournemouth. I never ever saw him as likely managerial material, although I'd heard over the years he was an excellent coach. While I never doubted that H, a typical lively Londoner, would always make a good living, my mate as a manager is something else – particularly when I remember some of the things he got up to as a player!

H always felt he was Ron Greenwood's scapegoat when things

went wrong. Most of the time he just moaned on to me in this vein, but on one marvellous occasion the worm turned. We played badly in losing at home to Newcastle on the day before flying out to New York for an exhibition match against Santos, of Brazil ... including the legendary Pele. Ron gave us a bit of a ticking off in the dressing-room after the game, and as usual included H in his remarks. Suddenly, H yelled, 'Ah, you're always picking on me!', snatched up a full bottle of beer and hurled it across the room, just missing Rob Jenkins's head as it smashed against the wall. There was broken glass and foaming brown ale all over the place ... and a very startled Rob Jenkins!

'No America for Harry,' we thought – but he was on the plane with us the next day.

I sometimes wonder if manager Redknapp has yet experienced the other side of that kind of coin, with one of his Bournemouth lads slinging stuff about in a temper at Dean Court!

H is not the only one among former mates who have gone on to become managers: two who were in that long-ago Charlton youth side have also done so. Keith Peacock had the job at Gillingham, while Ray Hartford manages Luton. Keith was a Charlton first-teamer for many seasons, but Ray, a big, strong centre-half, had only a handful of senior games there.

In our youth team days together Ray, a Kennington lad, was always full of fun and chatter. The best part of twenty years later, I sought him out after we'd lost 2–1 at Luton one season and we had a brief chat about the old days. Ray was very amiable, but I left thinking that manager Hartford is a rather more serious guy than I remembered him as that young hopeful from Kennington!

36

When they talk about 'hard men' today I have to smile. I honestly can't see anyone around now who compares with the likes of Tommy Smith, Norman Hunter, Nobby Stiles, Chopper Harris, Dave Webb or George Curtis . . . just a few of the really tough characters who are high on my list of such players. And of them Tommy Smith was always the number one hard man. If I ever had any doubts about that they vanished the night I saw him do a right John Wayne on a towering bouncer outside a Liverpool club.

We'd played a midweek game at Anfield. In those days of train travel, away games like that always meant staying overnight after the match. Some of us went out for a few beers at a club in the town which the Liverpool lads had told us about.

Several of them, including Tommy, were there. When the time came to return to our hotel and we went outside to look for a cab, the first thing we saw was Tommy eyeball-to-eyeball with this massive bouncer, who I can only imagine must have been an Everton fan.

Despite the other fellow's size, Tommy wasted no time on words, just waded straight in, and in the end had to be dragged off by some mates. After that, I did not need any convincing that everything they said about Tommy as a hard man was true!

It was as well for me that little incident came after and not before my own first encounter in action with the Liverpool star. They played at our place not long after I joined West Ham. Tommy came away with the ball over the halfway line, clearly intent upon a run at our goal. But then he let the ball run a yard too far ahead of him as he neared our box. I realised I had no option but to make a challenge – and they are the worst kind to have to make, when an opponent has lost control of the ball and is steaming in, desperate to get it back again.

Acutely aware of Tommy's iron-man reputation, I thought: 'Will he come in over the top on me?' Neither of us held back, and we both ended up on the floor with the ball breaking away loose. Tommy picked himself up, grinned at me, and got on with the game, perfectly happy. But that was Tommy Smith – a hard man, but totally fair.

There have always been the other kind in the game, who will come in with the raised foot. But they are not hard men – just the reverse, because that is the coward's tackle. And it is a tackle that is creeping more and more into the game these days. Once, you all knew the few you might expect it from. Now it happens with such an increasing frequency that something official should be done as quickly as possible to outlaw that career-threatening challenge.

The FA, the League, the PFA and the referees should get together and leave everyone in no doubt that those tackles that can break a leg will immediately earn a red card – no messing about with a mere caution.

Nobody should appreciate more than me that football is a physical game. That's the way I have always played it, accepting the give and take of knocks that result. If someone clatters me in an honest challenge I've no complaints. But nothing infuriates me more than the charlie's tackle which can put you out of the game for life in a split-second. It is something that's been discussed more than once at West Ham, and our representative Steve Walford has raised it on our behalf with the PFA.

I can't remember Tommy Smith ever making that kind of tackle – nor another noted hard man of his era, Norman Hunter. The Leeds central defender had a marvellous left foot and never hesitated to get forward. But I always felt he was often underrated as a player, simply because of that 'Norman bites your legs' hard-man image which made him the toughest of a very tough Leeds squad.

Like Tommy Smith and Colin Todd and several others, Norman also had the misfortune to be around at the same time as Bobby Moore. If it had not been for the presence of such a world-class rival, Hunter would have finished up with sixty or seventy England caps, no trouble.

For a man who won just about every possible honour going, he also suffers the bad luck to be most remembered now – at least, outside Leeds – for the error which helped scupper

England's hopes of reaching the 1974 World Cup finals.

Ironically, Norman was called up to replace Mooro, after the latter's own slip had enabled Poland to take a 2–1 lead in the first leg of the qualifying match on their own territory. England's captain and most capped player was left on the sidelines for the return leg at Wembley, which England had to win.

Highlights from that game have been shown on the box from time to time since, and whenever I watch Norman going in for the crucial tackle I always think back to that very similar clanger I made against Plymouth at The Valley in my own early days. If England had been holding a winning lead, the Leeds man would have had no compunction about putting the ball up in the stands. But it was still 0–0 and he was obviously aware that England, pressing hard, needed possession. And, just like me in that Plymouth match, he tried to nick the ball off his opponent, lost it, and Poland went away to steal the lead and finally get away with a 1–1 draw that was enough to put England out.

Even then, Norman was unlucky. For he'd had to come out on the right side of the field, so that his interception was made with his 'wrong' stick. On the opposite flank, I'm, positive to this day, that educated old left foot would have done the business just as he intended.

Wembley was also the scene of an equally mortifying experience for yet another of that era's noted hard men, Webbie – Chelsea's David Webb. To me, he was a real throwback, with that crew-cut hair and utterly fearless approach. Webbie was a great character, on and off the field. What character he had as a player was shown when Chelsea met Leeds in the FA Cup final at Wembley. Eddie Gray, my old tormentor, gave Webbie a shocking roasting, the like of which has never been seen before or since. But the game went to a replay at Old Trafford and, far from being demoralised, it was Webbie who got Chelsea's winner, turning up to score at the far post – the epitome of what he was all about as a player.

That brave little man, Nobby Stiles, was another about in those days who would run through brick walls for the side, and was one of the heroes of England's 1966 World Cup triumph.

All of these lads were pigeon-holed as 'ball winners', which they certainly were. But each could play a bit, too, and when they got possession they used it effectively, short or long, whatever was on for them.

Not all of the hard men then were defenders. I suppose our own Keith Robson rates among the toughest attackers I've seen. Robbo had one of the best left sticks in the business – but also an almost manic urge to get in among opposing defenders. I'm heartily glad I played with him rather than against him.

Reputations meant nothing to him. I remember him dumping Tommy Smith over the touchline in the opening moments of a match at Anfield – lèse-majesté if ever there was! After a split second of shocked disbelief, the Anfield crowd bayed for blood ... and Tommy got up wryly shaking his head at the thought that anyone could be that mad.

He was a lovely lad, Robbo, and a great mate of mine while at West Ham, even if I rarely understood his Geordie lingo. But he was definitely not the kind of bloke you'd want your daughter to bring home! He was always getting into scrapes of one kind or another, but had such a happy, carefree attitude to life and got such enormous enjoyment out of it that you just could never get angry with him.

I remember trying hard to get him in order with his betting. We all like a little punt, but Robbo regularly went over the top – usually on horses that fell over. So when, once, he pulled off a big win I demanded that he handed over the best part of it to me. I pointed out that if he kept his winnings they'd all be back with the bookies in no time, and it would be much better if I shoved it into an account for him, where it would make a bit of money and he could have some out if really desperate.

A bit to my surprise, he for once saw the sense in this, and that's what I did. But I might just as well not have bothered. Before the end of the first week Robbo was pleading with me to let him have some of it back again, and within a very short time he'd had the lot – and passed it on to the bookies! I told him what a silly b he was, but it was impossible to really steam into such a happy-go-lucky character. We ran into him again last season at Norwich, one of the clubs he played for after leaving us, and I was pleased to see he was still the same old large-as-life Robbo.

It was a real coincidence that another of the really good

friends I had at West Ham was also named Robson and also a Geordie. But that was the only similarity between Keith and Pop Robson!

The two could hardly have been more different otherwise. Pop was the typical family man, never happier than when at home with his wife and children. He was a tremendous player – that rare combination of goal-scorer and grafter which, today, has virtually vanished from the game.

Among other 'hard men' forwards I've faced I'd rate Kenny Dalglish high on the list. While not obviously robust, Kenny always knew how to look after himself, and was not slow to give you an elbow if necessary.

Kenny and his contemporary attackers learned their craft in a hard school. Tackling from behind was allowed far more in their early days than now, and riding those challenges without losing possession was no easy art to master without a readiness to give as good as they got physically.

While I've already shown I'm among those anxious to see the over-the-ball tackle stamped out, I also feel that, in some areas, players may be over-protected now. How often, for instance, do we see the good, old-fashioned shoulder charge? Properly used, as laid down in the laws, that was once a regular, legitimate ball-winning tactic. Try it now and the whistle goes. It was very much part of the armoury of such feared number nines as Nat Lofthouse, Bobby Smith and Ron Saunders. I suppose Fash is about the nearest modern-day equivalent, but for robust play he is way behind Alex Dawson, the old Preston centre-forward I faced a few times.

As I say, you got away with much more in those days, and Alex could be really intimidating, particularly to goalkeepers. A bull of a man, with a badly squashed nose as the result of his many head-first collisions with opponents, Alex seemed to make the very ground shake, the way he thundered about. And with that flattened hooter you could always hear him snorting and snuffling at 25 yards range – not a pleasant sound if he was roaring in up your back!

Alex made the most of his formidable appearance. I remember him once really putting the wind up Charlie Wright, the Charlton goalkeeper, in a game at Deepdale. 'Watch out,

Charlie – the next corner I'm putting you and the ball in the back of the net,' Alex said. I didn't blame Charlie for being terrified! The promise was more than enough to distract his attention. Whenever the ball was in the air around our goal after that, Charlie had more than half an eye on Alex. We lost 4–1!

But it wasn't all one-way traffic (that's why the chunky Alex had such a misshapen nose!). Goalkeepers did not rely on refs for protection. When they came out, they came hard, always with one solid knee raised, and it was your own fault if you copped that or if your head happened to be in the same general area as their powerful two-fisted punch away.

A lot of the excitement and incident which stemmed from such clashes has now gone from the game. The slightest contact with a goalkeeper brings a free-kick.

Don't get me wrong: I'm all for refs giving players the best possible protection, and nobody needs it more than a goalkeeper diving headlong for the ball among flailing boots or going for a high cross, off the ground at full stretch. But it seems to me the whistle goes a mite too readily these days. I watched Arsenal and Everton on the box last season and saw Gunners' big Irish striker Niall Quinn have two goals disallowed that would certainly have stood in my early years in the game.

Football is a game of physical contact. What's fair in that respect is well defined in the laws. If we go too far in the interpretation of those, however, I fear that the game – and the customers – will lose out.

37

With his utterly committed approach and tremendous will to win, Wimbledon's Vinny Jones is clearly a very important part of their team. Eleven players like that and you are definitely in with a shout ... as Wimbledon have proved. But while he is probably rated the outstanding hard man about in Division One today, Vinny is really only a pussy cat compared to some of those of the past that I've already written about.

I still got into trouble, though, when we met last season! Vinny's attempts to wind me up with little shoves, tugs and taps at corners and set-pieces, and non-stop verbals, literally made me laugh. I mean – it has to be a waste of breath for him to keep on about me being a has-been, an old man, and past it, after the years I've already spent listening to that kind of stuff. It probably never occurred to Vinny that I had heard it – and more – a hundred times before. He tried so hard, however, that I had to admire him. But in the end I just could not help turning round and laughing at one particular jibe ... which levity promptly earned me a ticking-off from big Fash!

For all his own robust style, Fash is a very nice guy. When he saw me grinning at his team-mate, Fash came over and, very serious, declared: 'I'm surprised someone as experienced as you should try to provoke him like that, Billy. I thought you would have known better.' By the time I got through trying to explain to Fash that I had not been doing that but was just honestly amused, that stinging rebuke threatened to disrupt my concentration far more than anything Vinny had been up to!

Fortunately, Vinny has just the right man to channel his energy and spirit the right way, our old striker Bobby Gould. Gouldie was an excellent dressing-room influence in his brief spell with West Ham, always chatting away about everything and anything, just the kind of character it's very handy to have about if things are maybe not going too well.

Listening to him on the box and radio a few times since he

became Wimbledon's manager, I've been highly impressed with the way Gouldie has handled himself. People invariably change quite a lot when they move from playing to managing – they have to. You can hardly remain one of the boys and be in charge at the same time. But Gouldie strikes me as one of those who have managed the transition very well and can keep a natural liveliness without losing authority.

It will be interesting to see how Vinny Jones progresses under his guidance.

38

When Bobby Moore left West Ham in 1974 and I took over from him as captain, I had no illusions about the problems of succeeding such an all-time great in that role. But I also knew I had to do it my way, because it simply wasn't possible for me – or anyone else – to lead the side in the same manner as Mooro had. Virtually the only similarity between us as players and captains was that we both strove to lead by example. Otherwise we were about as different as Trevor and me.

A world-class defender who set a record for international caps at a time when there was no shortage of really fine contenders for his place in the England side, Bobby rarely showed any emotion on the field. Whatever happened, he was totally unflappable.

My own emotions are never far below the surface and, whereas Bobby was never a great talker on the park, I have always had plenty to say and been quick to have a go at team-mates and gee them up.

When I first joined West Ham, I don't mind admitting, I was completely in awe of Bobby, almost too frightened to speak to him. He was such a great player I found it difficult to accept I was actually his team-mate, even though he was friendly enough and easy to get on with. I often felt that, having had Mooro come as an already established star to present awards to my Sunday morning side when I was about thirteen or fourteen created a kind of relationship I never really grew out of, throughout all the years I knew him afterwards.

I've never forgotten, for instance, the very first little incident between us, if you can call it that. We were playing at Sunderland and, at one point in the game, I suddenly saw what I thought were gestures being made in my direction by Mooro. I knew I wasn't at fault over anything and, hot-headed as usual, started mouthing across the park at him: 'What are you having a go for? Why are you picking on me?'

With a faint smile, Mooro continued to point my way, but

indicating that his target was beyond me. Immediately, it dawned on me, to my horror, that all he'd been doing was indicating to the linesman that the flag ought to have gone up for an off-side in our favour! I felt a right idiot, about an inch-high one, having mouthed off at the skipper without stopping to work it out for myself. It was a long time before I let my mouth run away with me again where Mooro was concerned.

To me, Bobby thoroughly exploded the myth that you could never be a good player if you were not quick – an idea that prevails now more than ever. When players are discussed these days, almost the first questions you hear is 'Is he quick' or 'Does he lack pace?' Mooro was not slow by any means, but neither was he greased lightning. In addition, he was average in the air and certainly not a fierce tackler. But his reading of the game and his timing enabled him to overcome this and develop into the outstanding player of the day in his position.

He played football as if it was snooker – always thinking not just one but two moves ahead. Time after time he would come away with the ball at his feet after nicking it with the minimum of effort just when it seemed an opponent had left him for dead – no thundering challenge which left the ball running loose, but a perfectly timed foot in at the last second to win possession clean as a whistle and leave himself time and room to move forward.

When he did that kind of thing on the edge of our box it was literally heart-stopping. You'd look and think he was in an impossibly tight situation, knowing if it had been yourself you would have been glad to slide the ball away, hopefully to a team-mate, or just clear your lines. But Bobby would emerge, cool as a cucumber, and almost casually drop a thirty- or forty-yard pass right on Hurstie's chest, almost without looking. So accurate was he with those long balls that it seemed like telepathy.

He was only human, of course, and playing that game meant that any rare mistake was almost always a howler. But for sheer consistently high standard of performance, Bobby had few rivals, which is why such excellent players as Tommy Smith and Norman Hunter could never hope to earn as many caps as they deserved. This naturally rankled with the fans up north, who could never understand why Bobby was invariably picked for England ahead of their favourites. Used to the hard, aggressive all-action styles of Tommy and Norman, they found Mooro's laid-back elegance like a red rag to a bull. Regularly, they showed how they felt with a chant of 'Where's your handbag, Bobby Moore?'

They might just as well saved their breath. Nothing flustered Bobby, and for all the effect that kind of baiting had he could have been stone deaf. I honestly cannot recall him ever losing his rag in a game. The response he gave was to play so faultlessly that it yanked the rug out from under the jeerers.

I remember once sitting on the train coming home from a game in Manchester, reading that city's classified football evening paper, where the report of our game read something like: 'Bobby Moore was a man among boys in the West Ham team.' A bit of a choker to see yourself put in that category, but at the same time I could not dispute the assessment, for Mooro virtually carried West Ham for a few seasons around that time.

In his position as England's captain, particularly after the World Cup victory in 1966, Bobby was regularly under intense pressure off the field, always in demand to do something or other. Very often it seemed almost as if he was public property. But Mooro handled all that off-the-field pressure in the same laid-back way he played the game.

Bobby adopted the same no-fuss approach to training. He just came in and did a thorough job – never working harder than when he'd been out all Sunday on some gruelling personal appearance. Keenly aware of the hard work he'd done to become such a marvellous player, he realised better than anyone that the only way to stay number one was by keeping at it.

We will probably never know the real story behind that ludicrous business in Colombia in 1970 before the Mexico World Cup finals, when it was suggested Bobby had something to do with the alleged disappearance of a costly bracelet from a jewellery shop in Bogota. Though he was not the kind of man I could say I ever got close to, I knew more than enough to realise that Mooro as a shop-lifter was about as likely as the Pope getting married. My immediate reaction was that the whole thing was a set-up. I still firmly believe that.

But whoever was behind it just did not know the first thing about Bobby Moore. They might just as well tried it on with Sir Alf himself, because trying to brand Mooro a thief . . . well, it was just a bad joke. And if the idea was to rattle him before the finals in Mexico it could not have been more misplaced. He knew the allegation was a load of rubbish, so being kept under so-called 'house arrest', first in Colombia and then in the British Embassy in Mexico City, would have quite the opposite effect on him . . . just like those chants at Anfield and Elland Road used to. I suspect he found it a welcome little respite from all the attentions surrounding him as captain of the World Cup holders, being tucked away for a time in the Embassy!

I chuckled when I read later in the book Greavsie did with Ian St John, *It's a funny game*, how Jimmy bunked over the Embassy's back wall, nipped in through the kitchen, and found his West Ham team-mate, while Mooro was being held incommunicado at that time. Jimmy reveals that the Embassy staff were stunned when they found the pair of them sitting there, having 'a good old chinwag'. Jim says he even persuaded Embassy officials to serve them tea . . . I'm only surprised the whole crowd did not end up having a party! As Jimmy goes on to add, Bobby came through it all with no problem and skippered England in Mexico 'in his usual impeccable manner'.

'A lesser man would have cracked under the harassment. If only England had half-a-dozen like him today,' concludes Greavsie.

My sentiments entirely!

39

Both as players and individuals you could hardly find two more different types than Trevor Brooking and me. Yet we became the closest of club-mates over the years. It was a partnership which surprised many – not least Trev's Finnish wife Hilkka, who once told Lyn she was totally baffled over how the pair of us were such great mates. I suppose it's the old business of opposite poles attracting. Right from the start, we got on like a house on fire.

The first time I ever saw Trevor was from the terraces at The Valley. I'd just made the Charlton first team and went down the ground one fine late season evening to watch our youth team play West Ham. I did not bother to get a programme so, while I knew most of the Charlton side, the visitors were all nameless to me. What the final result was I don't remember now, but I know Hammers murdered our kids.

Three of the West Ham line-up particularly took my eye that night. I learned later the trio were Frankie Lampard, Roger Cross and Trevor. Funnily enough, I can't remember ever mentioning to Trevor in all our later years together how I'd seen him in that youth game, and the immediate impression his elegant style made on me.

He made his West Ham first team debut very soon after I joined the club. But at that time he was not the peerless creator he subsequently became, and could not command a regular place. There was even talk at one stage of him leaving, and I seem to remember both Spurs and Newcastle were aired as possible destinations. But I have also heard it said since that the idea West Ham might part with him was merely a Ron Greenwood ploy to give Trevor the gee-up to make him fully realise his obvious immense potential.

One of the best aspects of Trevor's character was the way in which, while he never touched alcohol, he could still always fit in when the rest of us were having a drink. If we dropped in at a pub, Trev was quite happy to go along and, though staying firmly on soft drinks, would never be out of place.

With his grammar school background and mannered ways he was, of course, the target for plenty of stick from us. But it was always something he could handle more than efficiently. In fact, his sense of humour and ready wit usually meant he gave better than he got.

As a keen golfer, like England cricketer Ted Dexter, Trev was at one time similarly known as Lord Ted among us. Another time, when I joined him in the England squad, I found out they called him Hadders – after *Hadleigh*, a very popular TV series whose main character was a very up-market type, with the same head of black hair as Trev.

These, however, were just passing fancies, and to us Trev was always Boog. This tag dated from an early West Ham close-season trip to the States. We watched a lot of baseball during our six weeks there. Our base was Baltimore and the Baltimore Oriels were the local side. One of their fans' favourites was a guy called Boog Powell, a hefty, over-weight fellow whose running was definitely not his strong point. To do any good, Boog used to have to hit home runs. Otherwise, he invariably ended up sliding his considerable bulk along the ground over ten or fifteen yards, arriving at base in a great cloud of dust. In his early days, Trev seemed to spend a lot of time on his backside ... so we happily seized on Boog as his nickname, and it stuck for ever after. By the time Trevor retired, of course, the original reason for calling him Boog had long gone. That loping stride, the graceful elegance on the ball, made him poetry in motion on the field. But he remained Boog to us.

For all his style, Trevor was also a very hard man to dispossess because he shielded the ball so well ... and he was too big a lad just to knock off it. If ball-winning was not his forte, I never saw anyone succeed in bullying him out of a game, though a few tried! Some said he lacked pace. Well, he may not have been a greyhound, but Trevor could motor at deceptive speed.

In the joking banter that went on all the time between us, I'd tell him I would have gone on until I was fifty if I hadn't had to do so much running for him. But nobody was ever more keenly aware than me of his immense value to the side. Whatever I may have achieved tearing about all over the place, Trevor more than equalled in other ways.

I remember getting an equaliser once in a League Cup tie against Cardiff at Upton Park – a goal that came simply because I knew enough of Trevor's ability to realise the chance was on the way. He was out near a corner flag, with two opponents tight on him so that the possibility of a cross seemed slim. But I was ready to put my house on Trevor getting past those two. I ran forward into space, over came a perfect ball, and all I had to do was let it glance off my head at the back post.

That was the quality of the man. It explains how team-mates could reach what looked like a telepathic understanding with him – Pop Robson especially – because they had so much experience of how he could work his way through the most unpromising situations.

Mind you, while Trevor was always creative, I often nagged at him for being too soft in his early days. He would take some real stick in training without reacting. Frankie Lampard was particularly merciless with him, and I used to tell Trevor: 'Don't just let him do that to you – have a pop back.'

Later on, as his career progressed, Trevor became a harder player, physically and mentally, and anyone trying to take liberties with him did so at their own risk. It's my pet theory that this changed attitude dated from around the time Trevor developed business interests outside the game and from when he married and had family responsibilities.

But if he altered in some respects, one thing that never did change was the way it was always me who made the tea or coffee when we roomed together on away trips! I waited on him for fifteen years! Invariably first up, I had no alternative but to put the kettle on, make the tea, then wake him up, with his cuppa (one sugar) and biscuits beside his bed. I sometimes wondered if just once before he packed in Trevor might leap out of bed and say: 'No, let me do it this time, Bonzo!' But he never did!

When Boog made his decision to retire it affected me quite badly. Frankie Lampard was also nearing the end of his time, and when Trevor hung up his boots it left me as the sole survivor of West Ham's 'old guard'. I did not suspect then I'd still be called on for first-team duty four years later, and being the last one left from that mid-sixties starting-off point was definitely a funny sort of feeling. And, of course, after fifteen years I really did miss having Boog around, exchanging digs with each other. Those little mutual micky-taking moments usually ended the same way – with me threatening him with violence – because I had no chance of competing with the verbals!

At more serious times, Trevor talked to me about his decision to retire. My view was – and is – that he went a couple of years too early. His touch and vision remained marvellous, even if he could not get around quite as much, and they would have more than earned him his place. Perhaps, if we could have foreseen how standards would drop all round, Trevor might have opted to go on a bit longer. But he was positive that he wanted to leave the game while still a fine player, to go out at the top.

He still trains regularly at Chadwell Heath. Rarely does a week go by without him putting in one or two sessions there ... and, as ever, cheerfully returning all the rude remarks we throw at him. He also turns out fairly regularly for a Sunday morning side in the Brentwood area where he lives. But looking at the career he has built commentating on TV and radio, in addition to his varied business interests, who can argue that Trevor did not do the right thing in packing up playing when he did?

I suspect that kind of continued connection with the game did much to ease retirement as a player for Trevor. He must have felt it much more if he'd simply cut right adrift and concentrated on business. His television and radio involvement with football keeps him very much in touch, even if there's no substitute for actually playing.

I'm the first to appreciate just how fortunate I am to go on so long. There are days, I freely admit, when I wonder what the hell I'm up to, going out to train on a dark, freezing winter's day with a wind right off the North Sea cutting across Chadwell Heath; or when I lever myself out of bed in the morning ankles and knees cracking, and Lyn takes one look and demands: 'How on earth do you think you can go training today?'

But when I think of the possible alternatives – and remember that factory bench I hated so much – I know what a lucky bloke

Billy Bonds has been!

For all the aches and pains, which now take so much longer to ease out, the thought of having to stop playing scares me stiff. I know it has to end some time – but if I *can* go on like Stan Matthews did I'll be delighted. All along, I've said I will be first to know when it is time to call it a day. To be honest, I've expected it to happen for a long time now.

Every summer I do my weekly running without problems. But every pre-season I report back thinking, 'This is the year my legs are going to tell me I can't get through the training any more.' But so far they haven't let me down – a bit slower maybe, yet still able to keep up with everyone else.

Playing competitively is what it's all about, of course, and I love that as much as the day I started. But I know now that what I'm really going to miss is the day-to-day involvement of the club. Training is a serious business, but there's also a lot of fun with it. Then there's being part of a team, going on the coach to away games, staying overnight somewhere, the card school, the Friday nights at the dogs with your mates. If I ever have to give up all that, after so many years, it will take some getting used to.

40

The late Bill Shankly once declared: 'Football isn't a matter of life and death – it's more important than that!' Well, there was a time once when I would have fully agreed with Shanks about that. But not any more.

For many years you would have gone a long way to find a worse loser than me. When we got beat I'd come in after the game in a real foul temper. For the rest of the weekend I would be miserable and, if I didn't exactly have the hump with Lyn and the girls, I was definitely bad company. All I could ever think about in that situation was getting out there again and putting things right. The next match could not come quickly enough.

Yet, bad loser that I was, I did not go in for ranting and raving over defeats, or chucking things about in a paddy. Some players storm into the dressing-room after a reverse, cursing and swearing about everyone and everything. Others just sit in a corner, literally with tears in their eyes. Me, I just got out as soon as I could. But it would stay in my mind, and nobody was more upset.

Considering how hard I took losing for so long, I am surprised to find myself mellowing more and more, the older I get. Winning is still what it is all about for me, but if we don't win then it's no longer quite the end of my world anymore. As long as I am sure in my own mind that I have given all I am capable of – for the fans, for the club, and for myself – then these days I accept there's not a lot more I can do about it.

Defeats will always rankle, of course, but at least now I have a more philosophical attitude to them, and can go home and enjoy the rest of the weekend. Football is a living and I want to do it well, but I have learned there are more important things in life than losing a match.

Cup football apart, there are always games you want to win rather more badly than others, like the big London derbies where there's local rivalry and pride involved. Among these games, Chelsea have always seemed to be lucky opposition for me. I got my only hat-trick against them, and I also remember scoring in a 3–1 Stamford Bridge win when all of our goals came from the half-back line – Mooro, Tommy Taylor and me.

In my early West Ham seasons we had some marvellous derbies with Spurs, the best I remember probably being a 2–2 draw which was afterwards rightly described as a classic. How often do you hear that said about games now?

There were lows as well as highs in the London derby matches, and I never much enjoyed those with Arsenal who, around their double season, played it very tight and gave absolutely nothing away.

But to be honest I have always got more out of playing away games up north than down here. Even there, it's not quite what it used to be. But the Merseyside and Manchester derbies always had an atmosphere rarely matched in the south. The games we played up north seemed to generate a passion quite different to anything in the capital and, though results have not been as good, I've enjoyed playing at Anfield and Old Trafford more than on the big London grounds.

Obviously, playing at home is different. The most electric atmosphere I ever experienced was at Upton Park on those European nights. But given the choice of away grounds I would have to go for the north. Playing in front of forty or fifty thousand committed fans invariably sets the old adrenalin flowing for me, despite knowing they are all rooting for the opposition.

Intimidating? Yes, of course it is. But it's how you react to that highly-charged atmosphere that counts. Personally, it has always been added motivation to do well for me, and I'm only sorry there aren't more places like Anfield and Old Trafford, and Elland Road in Leeds' hey-day.

Put in a nutshell, I suppose my attitude is: if you can't play well in this kind of atmosphere, where can you?

And having the home fans yelling for my blood if I'm putting it about has never worried me. In that respect, I'm the same as Billy Bremner, who once said he only ever got bothered when the home fans were *not* giving him stick – because that meant he was not playing well.

Maybe it's different for refs and linesmen. They are only human, but until you've done their job it's impossible to know how much they might be swayed by a particular venue and its crowd. It's easy enough to believe it happens when decisions go against you at either Old Trafford or Anfield. I remember a penalty at Liverpool that had nothing to do with the fans' reaction – which, like ours, was one of total astonishment when the ref suddenly pointed to the spot. Then there was Mark Ward's indirect free-kick at Old Trafford which everyone except the ref thought was touched by Gary Bailey on its way into the net. I suspect, though, that we tend to recall those incidents so well simply because of where they happened. Over the years there must be plenty of other places where we've copped some funny old rulings, now forgotten because they did not make the same impact as they would have if it had been at Liverpool or Manchester United.

There's only one real reason why visiting teams have had so little joy on those famous grounds . . . the other side were better every time!

41

Only once in my career have I been handed the 'spying' job on forthcoming opposition ... and I have to confess I did not do too well!

It was a time when I was sidelined through injury. Geoff Pike was similarly out of action, and John Lyall sent the pair of us to watch West Brom play Villa, since we were due to meet the Albion soon after.

We drove up to the Midlands in Pikey's car on a very cold day, with snow forecast. There was a big crowd for a Birmingham derby, and Albion went one up. To all intents and purposes that looked like being the only goal. Villa just never looked like scoring, the way they were going about it. We were freezing and, when the snow started to fall with about ten minutes to go, Pikey and I looked at each other and I said, 'I think we've seen enough, don't you?' The snow was swirling across the ground, we were both thinking of that old journey back down the motorway, and Geoff agreed: 'Yes, I think we have.'

Pulling our coat collars up, we slipped out of the stand, dashed down to the car park before all the traffic started leaving, jumped in Pikey's motor, and were away, pleased to have beaten both the departing crowds and the weather before it got too bad.

We'd gone some way before we put the radio on, largely to learn our own score. But almost the first thing we heard was: West Brom 1, Villa 3! Villa had scored three times in those last ten minutes – after we'd gone!

'Oh, my God. What are we going to do?' we asked each other, and started preparing our excuses for the Monday morning.

We felt a right pair of charlies, going all the way to Birmingham and then missing out on the most vital part of the game. We thought about reading all the Sunday papers and trying a cover-up of a clanger, but quickly realised that would not wash.

So when we got in on the Monday morning and were asked to pin-point the Albion defensive deficiencies in those closing minutes, we didn't try to wriggle out of it. Red-faced, we admitted we'd done a bunk before any of the Villa goals.

John did not say much when he heard this. But he seemed to us to have a sort of quizzical look that showed what he thought of Pikey and me as spies.

In the end, though, we did not feel too bad about it at all. Both of us had noted, during the eighty minutes we saw, how eager Albion's defender Whitehead was to get forward. He'd been a pretty useful winger in his Bristol City days, one I'd faced often enough, and still had a taste for getting down the line. We included this as one of the main points in our assessment, and said when he made those forward sorties it left Albion with three at the back – and the opposition with the chance of knocking the ball over Whitehead into the space his attacking had left. John obviously used this point in his team briefing, because when West Ham played Albion they did just that and got a goal out of it.

But neither Pikey or me were invited to go 'spying' again!

42

Friday the 13th is a date some people fear the worst from. But in November 1987 it proved the complete opposite for me.

I went into training that day fully expecting to see my name on the reserve team sheet for the match against Chelsea at Upton Park the next day. After training, however, John called me into his office and said he wanted me in the first team up at Everton, and asked how I felt about it. 'No problem, John,' I said, thinking to myself: that completes the hat-trick ... another comeback – and once again against one of the best sides in the country!

I went home, where Lyn was expecting me for lunch, and told her, 'I'm off to Everton this afternoon.' I thought she would be a bit surprised, because I had not expected to be in the first team again. But she wasn't, and said, 'Before you go you'd better have a read of this.'

It was a letter from the Prime Minister's office, saying I was being considered for inclusion in the New Year's Honours List and seeking confirmation of my acceptance if any award was made. Would I!

There was nothing definite about it, of course, and we told only Lyn's dad and my parents, not even my brother and sister – just in case there was a disappointment. We pondered a little about even telling the girls, but did so in the end, and they both kept their promise not to say a dickie to anyone.

When the New Year's honours list came out – with an MBE for Billy Bonds – it was followed by loads of congratulatory phone calls and letters. One of the first was, naturally, from Boog, who'd received a similar award himself a couple of years earlier. He told me just what was entailed, and what a great day out it would be, particularly for Lyn and the girls.

Among the letters I had was one from Liverpool Football Club, which I thought a very nice gesture ... even though Kenny Dalglish penned a personal postscript which read: 'Congratulations. Now you've got your MBE, isn't it time you packed in?'

I also heard from Mrs Basford, whose husband Jock played such an influential part in my early days at Charlton. Sadly, Jock had died some time before, but getting congratulations from his widow and her family made me realise that my award meant a lot to so many people I'd been involved with throughout my career.

Another letter came from Johnny Hollins – one which I appreciated not simply because he and I had known each other, on and off the field, for many years. Johnny had plenty on his managerial plate at the time with Chelsea, and I thought it was particularly thoughtful of him to take the time and trouble to drop me a line in those circumstances.

Geoff Hurst, MBE, and Pop Robson were other old team-mates to write or phone congratulations, and I also had many, many letters from West Ham supporters. I've kept every single one, all carefully tucked away with the rest of the West Ham and football memorabilia which I have collected over the years – and which I know one day I will be very glad I preserved.

Obviously, I looked forward to what would be an unforgettable experience, the kind money cannot buy. But I admit I was a bit worried about what to wear on the big day. Morning dress isn't really me and, in the end, I was relieved to find out that a plain lounge suit was also in order, and I went out and bought a posh new whistle.

It was soon apparent, though, when I got to Buckingham Palace on the day, that Moss Bros had done a roaring trade in morning suits. The military were all spruced up in their best uniforms, but everyone else it seemed was in tails and topper.

Fortunately, there was just one other bloke in a lounge suit. Directly we saw each other we were sort of drawn together and stood chatting, giving each other moral support, for about 45 minutes before the investiture ceremony. 'I'm bloody glad you're here!' I told him – and he clearly felt the same.

Funnily enough, he turned out to be a lifelong West Ham supporter. A probation officer from Kent, he knew the club inside out and had recognised me immediately. He had his family there, all West Ham crazy, and I met them later and gave his boy my autograph.

Afterwards, I got a letter from them, enclosing our two FA Cup final programmes, and asking me to autograph them ... and signed: 'from the fellow in the other suit'!

Apart from almost being the odd man out suit-wise, we also had one other little crisis on the day. When we got to The Mall the police lined us up with all the other cars before we drove, one at a time, into the Palace forecourt. At the gates they look at your credentials and then pass you on a few yards to where a security check is carried out, well before you are anywhere near the Palace.

It's all done politely but very thoroughly. The security men told us to stay in the car while they shoved mirrors on sticks under it, and looked in the boot and under the bonnet. I handed over the keys and, luckily, they went to the boot first. Because I suddenly realised I hadn't the faintest idea how to open the bonnet! I had only had the car a few months, and all I really knew was how to put petrol in it.

'You must know,' declared a disbelieving Lyn as panic set in, while the girls watched from the back seat as their dad groped frantically about the dashboard and under the steering wheel – I mean, it was hardly the time and place to start referring to the driver's handbook! Luckily, my fingers found the right lever, the bonnet popped up, and the security guys got on with it before I was really embarrassed. But I suspect they wondered why I was quite so scarlet-faced as they waved me on into an interior courtyard to park!

After that little upset everything was marvellous, the organisation perfect, down to the smallest detail.

Inside the Palace, Lyn and the girls were ushered into the main hall, where they could watch the ceremony from. They sat there for about an hour and a half before I went in, and told me afterwards how the Queen came in with an escort of Beefeaters and a Gurkha guard of honour. All the time, a military band up in a balcony entertained the people.

While they were taken there, I was shown into another spacious hall, where the MBEs and OBEs were grouped – the knighthoods had a similar hall to themselves.

On the way I realised the Palace was exactly how any kid

would imagine it to be. Long, wide corridors, imposing marble staircases, massive paintings on the wall, huge glittering chandeliers. And at every junction an absolutely motionless Household Cavalry guard, with plumed helmet, shining breastplate and gleaming boots, each one staring straight ahead unblinking.

The equerries instructed us on just what to do when we received our awards, which was done alphabetically in groups of about eight at a time.

We were led from that hall to outside the door of the main hall and told, when our name was called, to walk in, bow, turn left, bow again, and then walk forward to where the Queen stood on a small dais, making sure to be close enough for her to pin the medal on.

'Her Majesty may or may not say a few words to you. After receiving your award, step back, bow, and then walk away,' we were told.

I had expected beforehand to be a right bundle of nerves, but it was only when Her Majesty did, in fact, have a few words with me that the butterflies really began! She asked how long I'd been playing football, and I told her, 'Twenty odd years, your Majesty.' She then said, 'And you've been with one club all the time, I believe?' I said, 'Yes, your Majesty' – which was wrong, but I didn't want to get involved with trying to explain about being with Charlton first. 'Isn't that rather a long time to be with one club?' she went on. 'I suppose it is, your Majesty,' I replied ... by now just desperate for her to stop and let me go, because I was so nervous.

Obviously, I realised it was a great honour actually to get to talk to our Queen. But I just stood there thinking, 'Don't say any more ... just let me get out!'

Afterwards, when it was all over, we went out into the Palace forecourt for official photographs. You can have an oil painting done from these, which we did, and it now hangs on the wall at home.

The American NBC network cameras were also there to complete a short film they'd done on me, and we also have a video of that as a further nice souvenir of a great day out. Altogether, it was a fabulous occasion, particularly for the children, who are never going to forget it – though I think young

Katie finished up even more eager to go for a meal in the West End than she had been to go to the Palace!

The medal is now with all my other trophies and I'm very proud about it. But really it is the day itself that means so much. There is no razzamatazz involved, just a simple, impressive ceremony which recognises much excellent work done by otherwise largely unsung people.

For instance, I talked to a lady in her late sixties who received an award after years of ferrying transplant organs about the country. Like the probation officer, she was also an avid West Ham fan. When I heard what she did I honestly felt a bit humble. I'm not just saying it to sound like a creep or anything, but I think a lot of people have done much more valuable things than play football for one club for twenty years. From that point of view, I always find it a bit surprising when the likes of me are included.

But having said that, it is a marvellous honour which reflects not just on me, but on the club, the fans, my club-mates and the game in general. I still went home realising that the day had been all about many ordinary people from all walks of life getting richly deserved recognition – and a whole lot of priceless memories.

I also remembered later that it was not the first time I had seen the Queen. When I was about eight we all got a day off school because Her Majesty was opening something or other in our neighbourhood. We were taken to line part of the route and stand waving little paper Union Jacks and cheering like mad as she drove by. We were particularly pleased because, once the royal cavalcade had passed, we rushed off to spend the rest of the day playing football!

The lads, of course, did not miss the opportunity to hand out some appropriate stick. Galey, the leading light in that department, had them lined up in a 'guard of honour' for my arrival at training the day the award was announced, all bowing like mad, and for a week or two it was 'my lord' instead of Bonzo. But that was their way of showing how pleased they were.

The MBE has to be exceptional, but there was another presentation which, for me, was a bit special, not least because it was totally informal, out of the blue, and done, as you might say, in my 'place of work'. It came after my first full League game in the 1986–87 season up at Forest in February.

We drew 1–1 – a good result there – and afterwards I was standing in the dressing-room, stripped to the waist, when our chairman Len Cearns walked in with another man, whom he introduced as his Forest counterpart Maurice Roworth.

Mr Roworth handed me a parcel and said, 'I don't suppose we'll be seeing you here again, Billy, so this is a little something from Nottingham Forest Football Club in recognition of everything you've done for the game.'

I unwrapped it and found a lovely cut-glass vase inscribed with the Forest crest. It was a marvellous gesture and took me completely by surprise. The vase now has pride of place on our dresser at home.

The Forest chairman had every reason to think his club had, finally, seen the last of Billy Bonds. But the following season I was still there when we beat them 3–2 in the best game of the campaign at Upton Park. I learned later that Mr Rowarth, in all seriousness, was quite apologetic to our chairman because they had not brought anything for me that time!

When the seamy side of football too often gets the headlines, it's a pity that kind of decent, genuine attitude is not better known.

43

Winning awards is something I enjoy as much as the next man. What scares me is when you have to go to the presentations!

Various Player of the Month newspaper awards which have come my way at times aren't so bad. They are usually handed over out on the pitch before a match, and it's all over and done with pretty quickly. But the really big presentations, made in front of a hall full of people, when you are expected to come out with a witty 'thank you' speech – they're the kind that put the wind up me.

Some years ago I ended up on the shortlist of six for the annual PFA Footballer of the Year award. This has to be one of the best, since it is voted on by fellow professionals . . . and who better to know? But from the moment I heard I was in the running for it I really suffered! I dreaded the prospect of having to stand up in front of such an assembly. Colin Todd – my old sending-off partner – Billy Bremner and three others I can't recall were also in the final half-dozen, and I just prayed it would go to one of them and not me. I can honestly say I absolutely dreaded the prospect of winning and having to get up in front of such an assembly and say something.

When I got to the London hotel where the function was held, the whisper was already going the rounds that the award was Toddie's. Nobody was more delighted than me! Once I heard this often enough to bank on it being correct, I could forget all my fears and settle down and really enjoy the whole evening.

Similarly with going on television or radio. I've done a couple of TV things recently, but I can't honestly say it's something I like doing. There's always a few bob involved and I suppose over the years I have missed out on quite a lot of dough, turning down appearances of that kind. But I don't regret it.

With newspapers I always try to co-operate as best I can, though I confess I've sometimes nipped out the 'back door' at Upton Park rather than run the gauntlet of the press – like after my one and only hat-trick against Chelsea that time. I find it all usually adds a bit of pressure you can do without, so I do whatever I can to avoid it.

When I am approached by the media I have always been ready to respond if they are talking about the right things. I've never been interested in just going in and slagging off other players. I don't think that's on. If somebody has had a public go at me – like when Albion manager Ronnie Allen called me a gorilla – I've usually just said, 'Well, they are entitled to do that, it's a free country', and I have never answered back because getting into slanging matches isn't me. Too many people now seem ready to blow their own trumpet, and I've always been taught that self-praise is no recommendation.

That's not to say I am indifferent to that sort of thing. But if anyone has a pop at me, my reaction is to try and make them have second thoughts by doing it out on the park, not in a newspaper. Ron Greenwood was fond of reminding us that the place to really hurt the opposition is the back of their net. Let anyone say what they like, but if you stick one past them they have no option but to swallow.

Those rules, though, have never applied for me during the action. I am ready enough then with the verbals if somebody starts trying to wind me up that way.

I remember one match-long exchange between Tony Cunningham and me in his Newcastle days. He is a big old lad who can take it as well as dish it out. In this particular match he gave me a right hard whack early on – hard enough to know he wasn't going to get through the rest of the game without getting a similar one back, with interest if I could manage it.

I think he was relieved when I eventually got him just after the interval. We spent the rest of the struggle really telling each other a thing or two. He was going to push my face in. I was going to do the same to his ugly mug. We were definitely going to settle it outside once the final whistle went. But when it did we both looked at each other to see just how serious the other one was – and immediately burst out laughing, shook hands, and went off with no hard feelings on either side, the bumps and bruises forgotten.

Another reason I rarely get involved with the press after

matches is that it's been a career-long habit of mine to make the quickest possible get-away once a game is over. It's a standing joke that I'm disappearing down the corridor with a couple of cans of lager before most of the team have started changing.

Again, this is not because I particularly want to dodge anyone, simply that I feel my day's work is done and I want to get back home as soon as I can – like most people. To players, the football ground is the equivalent of the factory ... and who wants to hang about there longer than necessary?

I sometimes suspect this routine rapid exit has helped me to go on so long. For it's kept pressures down to a minimum and provided me with the maximum amount of time to relax away from the game. Some players who get involved find their phone never stops ringing with requests for tickets and favours of one kind or another, and it all adds to the already considerable pressures just playing brings.

But my quick get-away act doesn't always come off – even if sometimes there is a 'delayed reaction'.

Last season in a mid-week reserve game at Portsmouth, Fratton Park lived up to its bogey ground record for me. We played badly and were deservedly stuffed 5–2. Next day John Lyall had the whole reserve squad in the away team dressing-room at Chadwell Heath and gave us a two-hour rollicking. We'd fielded a very young side the previous night and John did not pull any punches in reminding them how lucky they were to be playing football with a First Division club for a living.

I had to sit through it, too, but I would not have had it any other way. All John said – and the need to say it – I fully agreed with. And as I was part of a team which had played diabolically, why shouldn't I be on the receiving end, too?

44

The decline in all-round standards has certainly helped me to keep going at the top level for far longer than I could ever have dreamed of, even if the game is faster.

To some I'm just lucky, a 'natural' athlete who has always been able to take fitness for granted. That niggles me a bit! For me, there's never been any personal secret, a magic formula, for fitness – except hard work. If there was, I would bottle it and make a fortune. There are no short cuts to fitness and, while you may be fortunate to be born with a strong constitution, going on as long as I have has meant working at it non-stop. I really never have a close season. The summer break these days is short enough, anyway, but throughout it I put my running in two or three times a week, so that when I report back for pre-season training I have not got to start sweating off excess weight.

Every season now for years I've gone back to work wondering if the time had arrived when I would be found out, when the legs would tell me, 'That's it ... time to pack it in.' I look around at the young faces of club-mates who were not even born when I started, and wonder, 'What am I doing here again?' And for a few years now I have been careful to tuck into the middle of the pack when we set out on the distance work in the early days of pre-season training. But every time so far I have found myself moving to the front before long, the legs as good as ever, and coming home in front.

I'm first to admit, though, that it's all that much harder for me now. A few minutes of really demanding one-on-ones in the gym, with the ball flying back off the walls all over the place, I could once really enjoy. But these days I find it much harder.

When I go home now after training, a chair and a book is favourite whereas ten years ago I would be straight out in the garden, getting stuck into a few jobs.

Yet, if it does not come any easier, my attitude hasn't changed. The lads will tell you I still treat five-a-sides like competitive games. If I'm involved in one that is a bit half-hearted, with no tackles going in, then I get nothing out of it and rapidly lose interest. I would prefer not to take part.

Stamina is no problem. If you have looked after yourself properly and still work hard, that will be the last thing to go. The first, of course, is speed. Mine went years ago. But with legs, lungs and heart in good nick, I know I can still run all day . . . at a certain pace.

To some extent experience compensates for pace. You get to know the short cuts, the back alleys to run down, where to cut the opposition off, out on the park. But you must still be able to get around quickly enough. It's no use being able to tackle if you arrive ten minutes after the ball has gone.

With the pace of the game getting ever faster, I admit I was a bit surprised that kind of thing did not happen to me when I first started getting those unexpected first-team recalls.

Ron Greenwood was always talking about players getting the right habits early on, and I have good reason to be grateful for those that were instilled into me – particularly Bob Stokoe's insistence upon the importance of that early contact with the ball in any game. I still go for that quick touch, but the difference now is that I try more than ever for an equally rapid lay-off. Players are so fired-up in the early minutes these days that any dwelling on the ball at the start of a match will guarantee you being kicked up in the air! I look on that opening burst as a 'mad half-hour', and I wait until everyone is satisfied they've made their silly tackles before I try much beyond one-touch stuff. Even so, you rarely get away without being flattened a couple of times!

Where I have unarguably been lucky to go on so long is with injuries, especially in view of the kind of game I play. This has always been a physical one of tackles and non-stop running, which inevitably means a lot of wear and tear on joints. But while I twice feared my career might be over through injury and illness, I have so far avoided the kind of terminal knock that removes all chance of playing any more. I have seen enough promising kids have to retire through that sort of injury before their career has got off the ground to realise how very fortunate I've been.

45

The first time I ever played on plastic tops was in America back in the late sixties. I hated them. I still do!

The synthetic pitches now in use here today are a big improvement on those I first experienced in Seattle and Portland during one of West Ham's close-season trips to the States. But I have no more time for them now than I did then. I'd be happy if they were all blown up! The fact is they just do not provide a true game of football, and I can't see how they ever will, whatever progress may be made in design. The surprising thing is that the League ever sanctioned their introduction in the first place.

It's easy enough to understand why certain clubs adopted them. The commercial potential is obvious, and for clubs who are trying to exist on meagre gates for League games this is clearly a welcome source of much-needed income. If you can hire out your pitch every day all the year round you are probably talking about forty or fifty grand you would not otherwise get. In this age when football's commercial tail very much wags the dog, there are places where any other considerations will not carry much weight.

But allowing clubs to play their entire home League programme on a synthetic surface has to be out of order. Visiting teams are already under a handicap as the away side. Having also to face opposition who must be far more prepared for the vagaries of a plastic top is, to me, an unacceptable disadvantage.

In case anyone thinks this is simply sour grapes, I must point out that West Ham currently boast an excellent record on plastic, even though they dislike it to a man. I think we have lost only three times in something like ten or a dozen League and cup games. In that time we have had some good wins, particularly at Queens Park Rangers, whose pitch must now be the worst of the lot. But I can honestly say I did not enjoy one bit the games those successes came in.

Playing-wise, the big argument in favour of plastic has always been that the flat, even surface is much more conducive to a skilled, passing game than grass. To a point, that's true. But there are other skills in football – like tackling. And that particular craft suffers badly on plastic. Apart from the very real problem of bounce, tackling on an artificial pitch is severely restricted because you just dare not risk the sliding challenge, a legitimate tactic which is a highly important part of the ball-winner's business. Go in with the usual full commitment on plastic and you are lucky if you don't end up with third degree burns.

We found this out on that long-ago American tour. Paul Heffer, one of Hammers' centre-backs, made the kind of sliding tackle which would be run-of-the-mill on grass – and came out of it with a really shocking knee. The burn he suffered scoured his entire knee-cap, just as if he'd shoved it in a fire. That happened in the very first game we played on plastic out there. It was terrible luck for Paul . . . but it gave the rest of us an immediate warning of how different football on plastic is. Ever since then, whenever I have to work on a synthetic top, I know the one thing I must avoid is ending up on my backside!

But there are always going to be situations in such games when you cannot avoid going in at full stretch regardless. It happened to me last season in a reserve game at Rangers – the one in which young Gavin Peacock, son of my old Charlton team-mate Keith, played against us. In the course of it, I had to commit myself fully for a fifty-fifty ball, the kind of challenge I've been making all my career. I knew when I did it I was courting trouble, and sure enough I collected a burn which took a good square inch of skin off a knee.

All right, I might have done the same tackle on grass and caught a stud or a knock. But that's an acceptable risk, part and parcel of the game. Knowing you are almost certain to suffer a nasty burn every time exposed flesh makes contact with the ground is not. Like most teams, we now cover those exposed areas with a special anti-burn cream before playing on plastic. It certainly helps, but in no way provides full protection.

If it sounds like I'm making a song and a dance about it, I should add that those burns very often result in a nasty 'follow-up' infection. Medical research is still going on to try and discover just what it is in synthetic tops which leads to this, and to find an answer. Players are naturally wary of this risk, so it is not surprising we don't see too many really good games played on plastic.

The PFA, the players' organisation, seems to have kept a regrettably low profile about plastic pitches. They might yet have to take a definite stand against them.

Rather like the so-called 'wonder' drugs that appear in medicine from time to time, artificial pitches have not been used in this country long enough yet for a proper assessment. It will be extremely interesting in a few years time to take a look at the incidence of joint and bone problems among players who have spent most of their careers playing on plastic.

It's a fortunate footballer who does not collect knee or ankle worries over the years, anyway – they play on plenty of bone-hard grounds in either early or late season, or in the depths of winter. But the special hard quality of most plastic tops must surely lead to far more than normal wear and tear. Phil Parkes, for instance, is quite positive that his playing days would now be long over had he remained at Rangers and had to play on their pitch, instead of moving to West Ham.

We could yet see a High Court case brought by a player forced to retire early after a 'plastic' career and suing his employer for industrial injury!

But those factors apart, artificial pitches for me destroy the whole traditional validity of winning a championship in the English League.

With our season played over nine months, if a side finishes up top of their particular heap then they have proved they are the best for all seasons, equipped to master the widely varying pitch conditions met from late August to early May. A team that sets off like a runaway train in ideal early-autumn going often grinds to a halt in November's mud or slithers down the table in a frosty mid-winter.

Liverpool have long been the classic example of a squad who can play their football whatever the going. But last season, when they were on to set a new Division One record for staying unbeaten from the start and had to go to Rangers' wonky old plastic, I was certain it was the one place they would come unstuck. In the event, they won 1–0, but it was definitely not a typical Liverpool performance.

Kenny Dalglish has made no secret of his positive hatred of plastic pitches . . . and, after a right belting on Luton's, got only a general raspberry for his pains. But we felt just the same when last winter's fourth-round FA Cup draw saw us come out of the hat away to Rangers.

I don't mind admitting that draw really gutted us. We would have preferred anywhere on grass – even Anfield – even though we'd won in the League at Loftus Road a couple of weeks earlier. And, despite spending the week before the tie preparing on a plastic pitch at Basildon, we were well beaten on the day.

So, if that's the anti-plastic attitude at West Ham, how do we feel about our own splendid indoor ball-court? John Lyall worked very hard in having this built and turning the club's Chadwell Heath training headquarters into among the best there is.

There's no doubting that it has proved a great investment. But the kind of work we do on that plastic is carefully regulated. It is ideal for individual sessions, honing ball skills, and for sharpening up control and quick, early passing in five-a-sides. Yet it could never be a complete substitute for the real thing, which we do outside unless conditions are dodgy. For me, that is the only proper use for plastic in football – as a valuable back-up in bad weather and for concentrated skills work.

I have every sympathy with those clubs who put in artificial main ground tops to help compensate for falling gates, but I'm delighted the pendulum of opinion has now swung the other way. For, much as I love football, there's no way I could ever see myself watching it regularly once I pack in if the game had gone over completely to plastic.

46

Some of the best advice I ever had was given to me by Don Revie. I had better add that it was given also to something like seventy or eighty other players at the same time!

One of the first things Don did when he took over as England's chief was to hold a one-day Sunday get-together of a very large group of players he rated as international possibles. This included Trevor Brooking, Frank Lampard, Graham Paddon and me from West Ham. The whole crowd met at a Midlands hotel for what was really Don Revie's introductory chat as the man in charge of the national squad.

A marvellous record of success with Leeds had earned him the job, and I am sure everything he had to tell us that day was excellent football sense. But there was one sentence which, though it had little to do with playing for England, so impressed me that I've never forgotten it.

'Always look after yourself. If you take care of yourself physically, don't abuse yourself, then you can get an extra year or two in the game and earn some more money out of it,' he said. It might sound mere basic commonsense, but there's no better advice than that.

When you are twenty it is only human nature to make the mistake of believing it will last for ever. But an average career spans little more than a decade, if a player is lucky with injuries ... and those ten years just whizz by, believe me! One moment you have established a regular first-team place, the next you are thirty, wondering if the old legs will be good for a couple more seasons, and where all the time went.

In my late twenties at the time of that England possibles meeting, I was probably of an age to fully appreciate just what Don Revie, whose own career had been shortened by injury, was trying to tell us. Nothing about winning caps, honours or medals – simply emphasising that for footballers the good years are relatively short, and only hard work and self-discipline can prolong them.

After that one occasion I never figured in Revie's England plans. Not until he was succeeded by my old West Ham manager, Ron Greenwood, did I have another sniff of the international scene. But, if nothing else, I've always been grateful to Revie for that timely confirmation of my own approach to the business in living the right kind of life and working hard.

Revie was never able to achieve with England the success he had at club level but, for me, the tremendous job he did at Leeds puts him among the very best managers about in my time in the game.

Without wanting to take anything away from the present Liverpool side Kenny Dalglish has assembled – undoubtedly a great team – I was not sorry when they equalled rather than topped the Leeds record for going unbeaten from the start of a season. Leeds set that mark when the First Division going was much tougher than it is now.

Yet, if Leeds and Liverpool have been the outstanding sides I've played against, Brian Clough's record as a manager must rival anything that's happened in my twenty odd years in Division One. Though I have played countless times against his teams, I've never exchanged a single word with Cloughie, never met him face to face. Listening to him on TV and radio and reading his comments in the papers, I must admit that, early on, he nearly always provoked an anti response in me. But you can't argue with the kind of record he's got, can you?

His achievements with Derby and Forest have been second to none. From being not too sure about him, I now have nothing but the greatest admiration and respect for the man as a manager – for the way he goes on producing teams that can play the very best brand of football. He has to be the greatest motivator of his time, somehow regularly able to get much more out of individuals than they appear to be capable of and to make teams play to a level which is far beyond what seems possible if you analyse them man by man.

Should he have got the England job? Well, I suspect his greatest talent is for spotting and then exploiting young players with it all still before them rather than handling fully established stars, though he's done well enough with those at club level over the years. But there's little doubt that, if he'd been England's manager, a powerful wind of change would have roared through every nook and cranny of football's establishment! He is on record himself as declaring that he would want to be in total control of everything. That attitude, and his frequent controversial outbursts over the years, must have scared the life out of the FA.

It is hard to talk about someone you've no personal experience of, and whether I could ever have played for Brian Clough is another matter – not that he's ever sought my services, as far as I know. It seems he can be utterly ruthless sometimes, like when he has paid big money for a player then virtually discarded him almost immediately, punishing that player for what he must have felt was his own mistake. But, equally, he has always shown himself to be a man who will do it for you if you do it for him, and more than that no player can ask of a manager.

47

Bob Paisley surprised few people in the game with his comments last season on the First Division no longer being as strong as it was when previous Liverpool teams won the championship. After twenty years of playing in it, I've no doubts whatever that the overall standard has slipped.

You need only compare the leading clubs now to what they were fifteen or twenty years ago to realise this. Man for man, present day line-ups cannot rival the teams that were about when I first came into Division One.

Manchester United, Manchester City, Leeds, Arsenal, Spurs, Chelsea, QPR, West Ham – none of them now have sides as good as in those days.

If you doubt it, just turn up an old programme for any First Division game from the sixties and compare the names in it with the line-ups the same two teams put out now. Not too many of today's players would have got in a couple of decades back.

Why there are no longer as many quality footballers about these days is a question that has a lot of people in the business baffled – and worried. For in other respects things have improved. Training is much more intensifed these days than it used to be, and the general level of fitness definitely higher. But despite this there has been a very marked decline in the skill factor.

In my early Division One years virtually every side fielded four or five quality players – the best teams twice that number. With respect to my present-day colleagues, this is not so any longer. Take Manchester United: who of their current squad would keep out the likes of Bobby Charlton, George Best and Denis Law? Or Manchester's other club: can you imagine Franny Lee, Summerbee or Colin Bell not walking into today's City side? The same applies to all the London clubs without exception.

There are various theories as to why the game has stopped producing such numbers of quality players, why skills have deteriorated: organisation, work-rate, fear of failure, poor coaching at school level have all been put forward.

I don't pretend to know the right answer. But I certainly wonder if today's hundred mile an hour game has not curbed the development of individual flair. For Division One football is definitely faster, and possibly the high-speed action does not allow young players to become skilful. It's all chase and run and one-touch football, highly organised within a team plan. Even so, I firmly believe a Brooking or Best would still be clever enough to put their foot on the ball, slow everything down, and be as creative as ever.

I've not yet mentioned Bob Paisley's own club, Liverpool – and that's because they are the one outfit who have successfully maintained standards.

The first Liverpool team I played against had some really great players. Thompson and Callaghan on the wings, Smith and Yeats at the back, Lawler and Byrne full-backs, Roger Hunt up front. Then you got the seventies and early eighties side – the Keegan and Dalglish era. Over the twenty years I have played against them Liverpool have always been an outstanding, hard-to-beat outfit. Like Bob Paisley, however, I am not sure the present squad is the best ever, despite a runaway championship triumph, better all round than those I've just mentioned.

The really impressive feature of their long-running success is the way they've managed the tricky business of transition. When any club has a winning team the great temptation is not to change it, even though everyone knows the best time to do so is just after a title or cup success. At Liverpool, no matter who is manager, they have somehow always brought in two or three newcomers at exactly the right time, and they slot in so smoothly that whoever they replace isn't missed. Obviously, you have to buy the right players in the first place ... and that's down to good management.

There may not be anything especially perceptive in paying big fees for such as Peter Beardsley or John Barnes, but you have to be sure their particular talents will blend with those you already have. And backing your judgement on the potential of Ray Clemence, Keegan and Ian Rush, when all three were relative unknowns playing in lower divisions, is even more creditable.

Earlier on, I rated Don Revie's Leeds as, on their day, the best team I faced. But for sheer solid consistency nobody comes close to Liverpool. What they have achieved is a football miracle. Many clubs get together a good team for a period, but eventually have to break it up and rebuild. At Anfield the continuity has been so well maintained there's hardly been a hiccup in twenty years. For instance, to me it seems no time since we had to consider Mark Lawrenson as a very dangerous opponent. Now he's gone from the Liverpool scene, yet the departure of such an outstanding player caused hardly a ripple in the team's efficiency. That has to be the big difference between 'them and us'. Almost any other first Division club would be struggling to overcome the loss of a player of that calibre – like West Ham since Dev's injury problems.

There may be envy and jealousy over the way Liverpool have cornered the talent market lately, but what they have done is a great advert for British football. The saddest thing is that they, of all clubs, should be involved with the tragedy in Belgium. For years they have been marvellous ambassadors for the British game. Their supporters have been terrific – I've always found them great to play in front of – so they were the last you'd expect to be connected with such reputation-wrecking disaster.

48

The decision to retire from the First Division scene at the end of last season was not difficult – the hard part was accepting it!

I always said I would be the first to know when the time had arrived for me to finally hang up my boots. No way was I ever going to linger on, like a guest outstaying his welcome, until somebody else had to tell me I was past it.

When the 1987–88 season began I had few thoughts about figuring in the first team again, apart maybe for an odd game. Rising forty-one, I certainly did not anticipate that I would end up playing in half the League programme. Right from the start of the season I had it in mind that it would be my final campaign. I cannot have done that badly, because our fans voted me runner-up to Robbo as Hammer of the Year, an honour I appreciated as much as when they gave me the award the previous season.

Yet while fitness was still no problem, I was not happy with my form in the second half of the season which, to be honest, I found a bit of a nightmare. You set your own standards and, for me, there were not too many matches after Christmas when I came off the field at the finish satisfied I had measured up to mine and able to take pride in my own performance.

The irony was that 1988 should have been a great year for me. People came up in the street and congratulated me on the MBE and the PFA merit award. After a particularly black Christmas period results-wise, however, you did not need a crystal ball to realise it was going to be a close thing for West Ham to avoid the play-offs, at the very least.

The pressures of battling against relegation obviously had something to do with the dissatisfaction I felt about my own game. It definitely gets to you when things are not going well . . . don't let anyone try to kid you otherwise.

Fortunately, we scraped clear of trouble, goal difference keeping us out of involvement in the play-offs. Injury kept me out of the final two games, and I sweated it out along with our supporters as the lads showed tremendous character in that final home match win over Chelsea.

Allowing for the fact that, on the day, Chelsea were under just as much tension, it took a lot of bottle for our squad to go out and play with the fluency and freedom that brought a best-of-season 4–1 win – and finally allowed us to breathe again.

If that result erased our worries, though, I could not help recalling the win we gained at Rangers the previous January, when Dicko's goal was the only scoring effort of the game.

John Lyall came up to me in the dressing-room afterwards to say 'well done', and I told him I thought those three points could be the difference between staying up or going down ... I was that concerned about our prospects.

The following game we picked up another vital, if very unexpected, point at Anfield. But when we subsequently failed to win home games against the likes of Portsmouth and Oxford and also lost at Derby, it began to look as if we might have the distinction of going down after a season in which Liverpool, the runaway champions, had twice failed to beat us!

For me, relegation would have been even more shattering than it was when we experienced it before. Then, I still had time to help put it right. But if my career had come to an end on that note it would have seemed as my previous twenty years and more had been totally wasted.

Well before the end of the season I had opportunity to talk over thoughts of retiring with old club-mates who had already done so. Trevor agreed with me, provided I could get the sort of future I hope for. But both Pop and Crossie were dead against it. 'It's murder when you pack in – you miss it like hell,' they warned me.

Of that I had no illusions. You can't spend over two decades as a first-team player and not feel like a fish out of water when it ends.

In an earlier chapter I've gone on about the tremendous, surging thrill of playing at grounds like Old Trafford and Anfield, and of those unforgettable Upton Park 'European' nights. Such occasions I am sure to think about often in the future. But what players miss most of all when they finish is the ordinary day-to-day involvement of being a footballer. Even in the kind of unhappy season we had last winter, it's still a marvellous way to earn your living.

I've never ceased to look forward to getting in for training – there's always so much fun going on, endless light-hearted stick to take and give, however demanding the day's work might be. Then there are those card school sessions, often rowdy, on the coach to away games, and the enjoyable Friday evening 'routines' when it's an over-nighter. After twenty-plus years of all that, it's difficult to imagine life any other way.

Whatever I felt about my own performance, though, West Ham were ready to give me another contract as a player. With typical frankness, John pointed out that he did not expect that to be at first-team level.

It was gratifying to feel West Ham still felt I could be useful as a player. But I was in complete agreement that it wouldn't be in Division One. I'd have loved to go on to fifty if the old legs would have carried me . . . but it clearly would not be good for West Ham to have someone of over forty-two years of age still around in their senior squad. The club has some talented young players and it's time they came in and proved if they are to make the grade, as I believe they will.

From my own point of view, I wanted to go when, hopefully, I would not be remembered by many fans simply as an old guy who had slowed up. So, while I might have gone on in the reserves, I was not interested in risking yet another enforced come-back in the First Division.

Some urged me, doubtless well meant, to drop down the divisions for a further season or two, and possibly I might have done so. But that would have meant leaving West Ham. You might just as well expect me to leave home.

It's been a marvellous club to me in all respects – directors, managers, team-mates, fans – in good times and bad. I've never forgotten how, after one season of battling to stay in Division One, Brian Cearns, one of Hammers' directors, took the time and trouble to write me a line saying thank you for my efforts as captain. That was typical of the kind of personal 'family' approach I have always found at West Ham. With a living still to earn, I suppose I would, if necessary, have pulled on another club's colours. But it would have been very difficult.

Happily, it has not worked out that way. As soon as John heard I was going to stop playing he simply said: 'Well, we must see about a coaching job, Bill.' It was just the offer I had hoped for.

In the last few seasons I have done some evening coaching with youngsters at Chadwell Heath, when first-team requirements allowed. My group is the under-12s and I found working with them very satisfying. With kids of that age one thing you are always sure of is total effort – which is what I'll always demand above all else. I can accept lack of ability, but never lack of commitment.

Now I am in charge of West Ham's youth squad, which is how John himself began his managerial career after injury curtailed his playing days. Whether it will lead me along a similar path only time can tell. I don't know if I have all the many qualities needed to be a manager, even if ever the chance arose. But after all the years working with so many great players and listening to people like Jock Basford, Bob Stokoe, Ron Greenwood and John Lyall I have learned a lot. Now I have a chance to try to put some of it over to West Ham's youngsters and give back something to both a club and life that has been so good to me.

And football has been just that to the kid from Eltham who went to work on a bike in his early days at Charlton Athletic. Looking back, I would not change anything. Given the chance, I'd do it all again. Perhaps I could have made more financially out of the game if I'd bothered with agents and the like. Don't get me wrong – I have nothing against players who do, good luck to them, it's a brief enough career. But it was never my style.

Football has enabled me to provide the standard of life I wanted for my wife and family, and I will never regret spending as much time as I could with them rather than out chasing a few extra bob. I suppose it all comes down to what each individual's idea of happiness is. The record will show that my final League appearance for West Ham was against Southampton at The Dell on 30 April 1988 – my 890th senior outing. It will also reveal that my West Ham career ended as it began, with an odd-goal defeat. For on my début against Sheffield Wednesday at Upton Park on 19 August 1967, we lost 3–2, while in that last game at Southampton we went down 2–1. And, after all the ups and downs over the years, it's perhaps no surprise that Hammers were in the lead in both matches! I even managed to mark my final league appearance with a booking ... which some, no doubt, will regard as a fitting finale for Billy Bonds!

I also played through the game with a dodgy knee and a sore ankle. But, really, I've been very lucky to come out of it all without a serious injury, particularly considering the way I play, chasing about and getting a foot in and tackling. At times I have upset one or two out on the park, but it has, with very few exceptions, always ended with a handshake and mutual respect.

Over the years I have acquired a real collection of souvenirs, ranging from gold Cup-winners' medals to congratulatory letters from people I'm never likely to meet. All are very important to me and, one day, when I retire completely, I'll go through the whole lot, putting them in order, and remembering what a great time I enjoyed as a player. But equally important to me is knowing I leave the game with the respect of my fellow professionals ... more satisfying than any medals. Nobody can ask more.

For similar reasons this book may well disappoint those who maybe hoped to read mud-slinging, controversy and barbed comment. Perhaps I have been lucky, but the people I've met in football, team-mates and opponents alike, have not been the sort to provoke that kind of bitter outpourings from me. If the next twenty years bring me the same satisfaction and excitement as the last, I will be a fortunate man, indeed.

These concluding words are written not long after the curtain came down on my final season – even less following retirement as a player. When I told Lyn I was packing in, she promptly said: 'You wait until pre-season work starts ... you'll be back there, eager as ever, and wishing you were still playing!'

'If I am,' I told her, 'just remind me how low I was towards the end last year.' But, even as I said it, I suspected she would prove right.

APPENDIX

Billy Bonds Career Record

Charlton Athletic

	Appearances FL	Appearances FAC	Appearances LC	Goals FL	Goals FAC	Goals LC
1964–65	13	–	–	–	–	–
1965–66	40	1	2	–	–	–
1966–67	42	1	1	1	–	–
	95	2	3	1	0	0

West Ham United

	Appearances FL	Appearances FAC	Appearances LC	Appearances ECWC	Goals FL	Goals FAC	Goals LC	Goals ECWC
1967–68	37	3	2	–	1	–	–	–
1968–69	42	3	2	–	1	–	–	–
1969–70	42	1	2	–	3	–	–	–
1970–71	37	1	2	–	–	–	–	–
1971–72	42	4	10	–	3	–	2	–
1972–73	39	2	2	–	3	–	–	–
1973–74	40	2	1	–	13	–	–	–
1974–75	31	8	3	–	7	–	2	–
1975–76	18(1)	–	5	9	1	–	1	2

1975–76	18(1)	–	5	9	1	–	1	2
1976–77	41	2	3	–	3	–	–	–
1977–78	29	3	–	–	1	1	–	–
1978–79	39	1	1	–	4	–	–	–
1979–80	34	5	9	–	1	–	–	–
1980–81	41	3	8	6	–	–	1	1
1981–82	29	2	4	–	1	1	–	–
1982–83	34	1	4	–	3	–	–	–
1983–84	27	1(1)	2	–	–	–	–	–
1984–85	22(3)	–	4	–	3	–	–	–
1985–86	–	–	–	–	–	–	–	–
1986–87	17(4)	4(1)	3(2)	–	–	–	–	–
1987–88	22	2	–	–	–	–	–	–
	663*	48	67	15	48	2	6	3

Key: FL – Football League; FAC – FA Cup; LC – League/Littlewoods Cup; ECWC – European Cup-Winners' Cup. Appearances as substitute in brackets. *A club record.

Other games: 1973–74 Watney Cup (1 app.); 1974–75 Texaco Cup (3 app., 2 goals); 1975–76 Anglo-Italian Cup (1 app.); 1980–81 Charity Shield; 1986–87 Full Members' Cup (1(1) app.).

Club Honours

European Cup-Winners' Cup runners-up medal (1975–76 vs. Anderlecht 2–4); FA Cup winner's medals (1974–75 vs. Fulham 2–0 and 1979–80 vs. Arsenal 1–0); League Cup runners-up medal (1980–81 vs. Liverpool 1–1 (aet), 1–2); Division Two championship medal (1980–81).

Personal Honours

MBE (1988 New Year's Honours List); PFA Merit Award (1988); PFA Footballer of the Year nomination (1979); Hammer of the Year (1970–71, 1973–74, 1974–75, 1986–87 and runner-up 1968–69, 1969–70, 1987–88).

Index

BB stands for Billy Bonds.

Index

Index